D1715753

Choosing to **WIN**
With Financial
Freedom

Josh Patton

Walnut Creek Publishing

Josh Patton

.

Printed in the United States of America
First Printing, 2018

Walnut Creek Publishing
P.O. Box 1832 Hillsboro, OH 45133

Designed by 99Designs.com

ISBN-13: 978-0692122167

Josh Patton

Dedication

I dedicate this book to my wife, Felicity, who married me when I had nothing, and helped me realize that TIME is our most valuable asset.

CONTENTS

Introduction

INTRODUCTION

I want to start off simply. This is not a "get rich quick" book or scheme, but rather, a lifestyle change that will help you on the path to becoming financially free. If you're looking to be an overnight millionaire, play the lottery; this book is not for you. This book is a collection of disciplined thoughts and ideas that have proven, with time, to make many people financially successful.

The idea of this book is to give individuals, who are willing, a better sense of financial stability and an achievable financial freedom. This book will introduce you to money management, debt uses (good debt vs bad debt), what compound interest is and how it works. We will also take a look at the stock market; mutual fund markets, what an asset is vs. a liability and what are acceptable expenses.

We will dig deeper into why giving back is a large part of financial success and how almost any working person, with persistence, dedication, and time, can become a millionaire This is also not a book with new groundbreaking ideas. This book is actually really simple. It will show you different areas of money, what it is and how it can actually work for you rather than against you. Ultimately, the choice is yours.

If you follow the concepts of this book, be ready to be made fun of. Be ready to be ridiculed. Be ready to change your mindset and be ready to change your life.

You may wonder why anyone would make fun of someone who is trying to better themselves and I agree, it's a valid question. However, I believe the answer is relatively simple. I believe most people don't want you to do better than they. I believe they want you to stay stuck in this lifestyle of living week to week, paycheck to paycheck and flooded with debt, just as they are. And, when you change what you are doing, they don't like it. It's almost like you throw the world off its axis by going against the "social norm."

This book will also give you a look into how to break bad financial habits and be more content with what you have. It will help you realize that "stuff" is not what life is all about.

You may hear words in this book that you haven't given much attention to before, like mutual funds, stocks, dividends, compound interest, investments and so on. But, know one thing. This book will help you realize that your money is a tool and it can actually work for you. This book will help you realize that financial freedom is achievable by just about anyone that is willing to try.

CHAPTER 1
WHY BEING SMART WITH MONEY
IS IMPORTANT IN YOUR LIFE

Back in early 2001, I had it all figured out. I was making a decent living as a plumber and life was good. My wife and I had bought our first house and we were living the American dream. The house had a beautiful setting on ten acres with a full basement and a pond. I had a newer Jeep Wrangler and all the toys I could ask for. We had it all. I mean, we had our house payment, a car payment, credit card debt, and owed on basically everything we had. We spent money like we had it. It was great! NOT!

It's so funny because at that time in our lives, people were thinking we had achieved at least some sort of financial success. I mean, we were very young (me twenty and my wife eighteen) and had bought our first home. We had decent cars and a good job. What more could anyone expect of us? The funny thing is, we had absolutely no savings and not a penny in the bank and were actually on the brink of bankruptcy.

At this point in my life, I had never had anyone who was great with money teach me anything about it. How money works, how it can be used as a tool or, even what smart spending was. I am sure a lot of people reading this right now are thinking "it's money; you make it, you spend it, and that's it. It's not that hard." And that's exactly how I thought about it at that point in my life. All I knew was the amount I had coming in every single week and in my mind, there was never any end to it. We were the epitome of living paycheck to paycheck.

You know, when you look back, hindsight is always 20/20. I mean, it's so easy now to say, "what if" or "I wish", but the truth of the matter is you can't change the past. You can only change the present, which will, in turn, alter your future. I love the one quote I read from Einstein that defines inanity like this: "Insanity is doing the same thing over and over again and expecting different results."

It's almost as if everyone can see what they are doing wrong, and they might even go as far as complaining about it, but they never make a change. They never decide to fix it. They just keep doing the same thing over and over and have the same complaints throughout their lives. It's an unfortunate repetitive cycle that we continue throughout our lives until we no longer exist unless, of course, we change.

So, you ask me: why is being smart with my money important? Why can't I just be happy, live paycheck to paycheck, pay my bills and live my life?

I mean, we are all going to die anyway, and what's the difference if I die in debt? I don't have to pay it, right? That's someone else's problem. And if I go through life saving, then maybe I'll never get what I want.

Wouldn't I be better off to get what I want now, spend my money and at least I'll die happy?

These are all things I've heard over and over again. Unfortunately, it's just not that easy.

Living in debt and living broke (paycheck to paycheck or worse) is not only financially irresponsible, it is actually unhealthy. I mean think about it. When you choose (and yes, I said *choose* because I believe wholeheartedly it is a choice in most cases) to live broke you are creating health issues caused by stress that you shouldn't have.

Stress is one of most serious causes of many diseases from heart attacks, cancers, depression and the list goes on. Wouldn't it be nice to think you could stop this? Oh wait, you can. We never think of bad money management affecting our health, but unfortunately, it affects our lives in more ways than we could ever realize.

The leading cause of divorce in the United States of America is money issues in the home. Money issues cause fights, which lead to stress, which lead to resentment and so on. An article from CNBC, written by Kelley Holland, says it this way:

Finances are the leading cause of stress in a relationship, according to a survey of people in a relationship or partnership released Wednesday by SunTrust Bank. Some 35 percent of all respondents experiencing relationship stress said money was the primary cause of friction. Among respondents with relationship stress aged 44 to 54, 44% said money was the primary cause.

(https://www.cnbc.com/2015/02/04/money-is-the-leading-cause-of-stress-in-relationships.html)

"Money really touches everything. It impacts people's lives," said Emmet Burns, brand marketing director for SunTrust.

Money and stress do seem to go hand in hand for many Americans, whether they're in relationships or not. A study released earlier this week by the American Psychological Association found almost three-quarters of Americans are experiencing financial stress at least some of the time, and nearly a quarter of us are feeling extreme financial stress.

Wouldn't it be nice to go home at the end of the day and not have to worry about if you can afford your bills for that week, that month or even that year? I know a lot of people are thinking "sure" but that's never going to happen. And with that attitude, you are correct my friend, it never will.

Each of us only has so much time on this earth. Not a single one of us knows the exact moment we will be taken from the earth or how much time we have left. But we should at least, while we are here, try and make the best of it. (And I don't mean spend like a drunken sailor). I mean actually have a purpose for your life. Have a purpose for who you are, what you do, how you spend, how you save, and who you love. Leave a legacy worth something!

Only So Much Time and Money

I was actually talking to one of my best friends this morning before sitting down to write this and I said something about not having the time to do something else. His response is something I've actually said myself many times. He said; "we all have the same twenty-four hours in a day, it's what we chose to do with that twenty-four hours that makes us have no time." Talk about a slap in the face! But I couldn't agree more. Priorities are key to being successful. I mean, think about it. We only have so much time each hour, each day, each month and each year. And yet, it seems like everyone wants a piece of it. And unfortunately, we tend to give up our time to someone way too easily.

I know it's a weird comparison, but there are 86,400 seconds in each day. That sounds like a lot when you throw it out like that. I mean just think if you had $86,400 each day. Life would be great, right? It could be, but what if you start letting people control your $86,400? Think about it; people are after your time just as much, if not more, than your money. I mean each hour you give away to something or someone costs you 3,600 seconds. Again, think if that were $3,600. So, if you work eight hours a day you just gave away 28,800 of your seconds (I'm not saying don't work, just saying some of our time is given away for us no matter what.) And if you sleep another eight hours (I never sleep that much. I always tell my wife I can sleep when I'm dead. She really hates when I say that). You just gave away another 28,800 of your seconds. That means you only have 28,800 seconds left. What about the kid's activities, homework or, getting dinner ready. Then we have cleaning the house, watching TV and of course Facebook. So, if you spend another six hours or so doing all of those things you now only have two hours or 7200 seconds left. I mean, in a grand scheme, that is simply not that much time left. And that's if no one else has taken your time for another project or use.

Now don't get me wrong. I am not saying "Stop" sit on the couch, grab the nearest bag of Cheetos® and give up. But rather I am saying be mindful of who you volunteer your time to and make sure it has a solid purpose. You wouldn't (or shouldn't) just give your money away with no meaning. I mean you wouldn't walk down the street and just throw it on the sidewalk. Or you wouldn't pay $3600 to watch an hour of the TV, so why would you be so irresponsible with your time? I believe we should all look at our time as being as valuable (or more valuable) than money. And I bet if most of us received $86,400 every day we wouldn't even consider giving up $3600 an hour to waste on things like TV, social media or video games.

When you do anything with your time it must have a purpose. If you volunteer your time, it must be for a cause you believe in. It doesn't mean everything you volunteer for should make you money or profit somehow. It simply means making sure it is a cause in line with your goals, beliefs, and fits your schedule.

Now I know some of you are sitting there "mind blown" that I would even have the gall to make a comparison of time to money and seconds to dollars. But, here is the thing. I can always make more money, but I can never make more time. So yes, I make an extreme comparison for an extreme circumstance. In my mind, my time is worth way more than money could ever be. Even if you die as the wealthiest human that ever walked the earth guess what? You still died! Time is worth more than money. It's that simple.

I love this one quote by Barbara Bush that says it this way:

"At the end of your life, you will never regret not having passed one more test, not winning one more verdict or not closing one more deal. You will regret time not spent with a husband, a friend, a child, or a parent."

No matter what, people will take advantage of you if you allow them to. That means they will take your time and money. And like I said, we only have a limited amount of each (even if you are super wealthy.) Money you can make more of; time you cannot. So, I am a lot more apt to donate money than time. Not because it's easier, but because as I said I can always make more money and I try to use my time in the wisest ways possible simply because it is irreplaceable. Life is simply too short to just give it away. Make sure each second of your day has a purpose. Otherwise, it is being wasted.

Set Good Examples

When I was young I didn't have anyone that really directed me with money. My parents were (and still are) some of the greatest people I know. My dad is probably the hardest working man I have ever known on this earth. Even at sixty years old, he could outwork me physically any day of the week. And my mom is the kind of person that always puts herself last and everyone else first. When I watched her with my aunt as she was dying, I truly then began to see how selfless my mother really is. They are great parents and I could never ask for anyone better than them.

With that being said, their money management skills were not so great. They have been in and out of bankruptcy multiple times over the years and just simply never got a true grasp on their finances. Being great people doesn't make you a great financial success. Being a financial success takes hard work and dedication. It also takes time. I didn't learn this as a kid and it took my own failures to realize.

My wife and I have three little girls. Well, I guess they are not so little anymore at fifteen, thirteen, and nine. I want to show my kids what I now know and what I have learned. I want them to see that even at their current ages they can make their money work for them. And to understand that time is one of the key variables in being financially free. I didn't learn this myself until many years later as an adult.

Teaching our kids about money should be a priority. Not so they can become millionaires and billionaires without a purpose, but so they can give back in a fashion that no one else can. So, they can create their own legacies by helping others and making dramatic changes in our world. So, they can continue with smart money choices and pass it on to their children. So, they can see the value in hard work and discipline. So, they can understand the value of their time and who and what to donate it towards. And so they can "live a life that is like no one else." (A quote from Dave Ramsey)

I know some of you just read that last sentence and are thinking "here we go, this guy is about to tell us about all the stuff he would like his kids to have that he didn't." Nope, that is not it at all. When I say live like no one else, stuff has nothing to do with it. Most people, whether they have the money or not, act and live like they do. (We'll get more into that in the next chapter.) However, I want my kids to live a more free and purposeful life. I want them to have less stress, be healthier, have a happy marriage, and be financially free.

There simply is a true freedom that comes from being smart with money. An obvious one is a financial freedom and another one is the freedom of your time. It allows you to take more vacations, spend more time with family and dedicate your time to things that are truly important in life. And I don't mean "stuff." Once you achieve this level of freedom you can't imagine ever going back to a lifestyle that is different.

We must be wise with our money. Not only is it important for a long, happy, stress-free life, it is crucial. Being wise with money and time is the key elements in the goal of becoming financially free. They are both factors that will allow us to live, serve and cherish all the seconds in life we are given.

It has to start with us. No one else will do this for us. It is time to stand up and make a decision. It is time to do this for yourself and do this for your freedom!

CHAPTER 2
BREAKING BAD HABITS IS HARD

Bankruptcy Is No Way Out

I remember when my wife and I first got married. I was *the* uncle at every Christmas, every birthday party or anytime there were presents that everyone loved. I would always buy the best gifts, bring the most food, have the nicest cars and be dressed the best. I was the man! So I thought. On the surface, everything looked great. I mean who wouldn't want all the "stuff" I had. We were killing it.

The only problem is we were not. We were drowning in credit card debt and barely keeping our heads above water. Even though I had a good job and even made decent money for that time in my life, we were living paycheck to paycheck and even less. By that I mean we were spending way more than we actually made. We were spending tomorrow's money today and were heading down a path of financial ruin. We spent money like we had it; the only problem was we had nothing!

Well, like clockwork, we picked up the tradition in my family of filing for bankruptcy. I still to this day remember it like it was yesterday. I was so ashamed as I walked into the fifty-story building in downtown Cincinnati to go talk to the attorney. He said it will cost you $1,000 and we will get all your debt wiped away. I didn't have a $1000. I didn't even have $100 extra dollars. With ill advice I borrowed the $1,000 on a credit card to pay the attorney. It didn't matter anyway, right? I mean, all my debts were about to be wiped clean. All I had to do was file and I was ready for a new slate of spending and starting the trend all over again.

As I spoke with different family members and told them what I was about to do, every single one of them said it was the best solution. They said that I should wipe my debt clean and move on. They are big companies anyway. I mean, it's their fault they lent me the money on multiple, unsecured credit cards. I just applied, they could have said no, right? I'm completely ashamed today that this was the mindset I had back then. I had the perception that they had more money than me and they were a big company, so they deserved to take the hit. It wasn't my responsibility to pay them, they should have never loaned me the money.

So, after a little bit of thinking about it (and I truly mean a little bit), I decided to follow in the footsteps of my family's finances and file for bankruptcy. I had convinced myself that this was the only way out. That if I didn't do this I would be in debt forever and never be able to live a happy life. I had bought right into the lies that most people do. I was giving up.

Do you want to know the crazy thing? The crazy thing is my credit score when I filed bankruptcy was 780. I had great credit and hadn't even been one day late on any payment at all. Yes, I was spending like a drunken sailor, but even though I had no money saved I always found a way to scrape up the money and pay.

And even worse than that, I actually only owed about $12,000 in credit card debt. That's right. I was willing to destroy mine and my wife's financial future over $12,000 that I had spent.

I know some of you are thinking right now, "$12,000, that's a lot of money. I would have filed as well." But to be honest, $12,000 is nothing in the grand scheme of life. I mean sure, it's a lot of money. But, is it enough to destroy your financial future over? Or is it just the easy way out? I can tell you with certainty, for me and for almost everyone else; it is the easy way out.

Like I said before, I had a great job at that time in my life. So good that the year I filed for bankruptcy I received a $1,000 bonus that summer and a $5,000 Christmas bonus. When I received both of those bonuses I was living on top of the world. But do you think I took any of that money and decided to pay off my debts and not go bankrupt? You guessed it. NOPE! I filed anyway.

My point is this. It wasn't like I didn't have the opportunity over the next two or three years to pay that money back, because I did. It was simply easier to spend my money on what I wanted and then let the credit card companies take the hit for my misfortunes (bad financial mistakes.)

I remember getting that $5,000 that year. The first thing I did was try to figure out how I could spend it. I remember going out and buying an old CJ7 Jeep. I wanted to fix it up just so I could have another toy for people to see. Even though I already had a motorcycle, two other cars and all sorts of other "toys" none of that was enough. Now I would be satisfied, right?

Wrong again. I spent money like it was unlimited, I had filed bankruptcy and I had no interest in changing my ways.

Even though I know bankruptcy seems like the easy way out (and I guess it kind of is if you just want to give up) it's most definitely not the best way. I wish to this day that I would never have filed for bankruptcy. I destroyed my credit, my finances for ten years and put a big dent in my pride. And to this day, I regret ever doing it; $12,000 seemed like a lot of money back then, but I could have figured out a way to get out of it.

I could have quit spending and buckled down and within a two to three-year period been debt free. I could have avoided bankruptcy, but I didn't want to. I didn't want to change the way I was doing things. I wanted to blame someone else because that was easier.

If you are facing any sort of issue like this in your own finances right now, I ask you to take a step back and think about it for a second. Don't make the mistakes I did. Just because it seems easy and just because you may have people telling you to do so, it doesn't mean it's the right way to go. There are other ways to get out of debt and other ways to solve your financial situations. Yes, it will take harder work and it will take time and dedication, but in the end, it is worth it. You will still have your credit, your financial future, and your pride.

You will also come away with the experience of having to get through a tough time. Where you had to spend less, work harder, save more and maybe even take on a second job or other work on the side. These are things you will never learn in any school and will never learn through a bankruptcy. You only learn these things through experience and changing your ways. You may ask "well, how did you learn it then?" I mean, I filed bankruptcy, right? And it worked out for me. Well, not necessarily. After I filed my wife and I almost ended up in the same situation we started in.

Going Back Down the Same Path

Over the next two or three years after filing bankruptcy, my wife and I continued to spend just as sporadically as we always had. We ended up selling our house and bought a new one in the 2005 housing market peak and we even made about $15,000 profit on the sale. (Kind of ironic that we made $3,000 over what we had filed bankruptcy on just a few years earlier.) So, we decided to take that money and buy all new furniture, lawnmower, appliances and again went right to spending like drunken sailors. The only exception was this time we were spending *our* money. So, it was different. Well, not so fast. After we blew through that money, we refinanced the new house a year later and took out another $15,000. We decided to buy a new used truck with that money (so now I was paying thirty years on a truck) and then blow whatever was left. Well, we sure kicked that financial goal's ass. I mean, if we actually had a list of how to do everything wrong we would be nailing it!

Now comes the good part! Our new loan through whatever mortgage company we used at that time was a 7.9% interest only loan (no principal at all) with a two-year balloon. The guy really swindled me into that one, but seeing how I just filed bankruptcy not too long before, I just wanted anyone to lend me money. But what that meant was that in two years we had to refinance for the entire amount of the original loan. So, we basically were renting the house because no principal came off the loan at all. Well, guess what happened next? The 2008 recession. Not such a great time to try and refinance a house that is now worth $30,000 less than we owe on it. Here we were once again only three or four years later staring down the barrel of financial ruin. Have I learned nothing!

So, I start trying to talk to any bank that would listen and convince them to take a chance on me. I begged them to refinance our loan, so we didn't lose our house. But the banks looked at me like I was stupid. They had seen that I had just filed bankruptcy a few years earlier and didn't even blink as they said NO.

Just when I thought it couldn't get any worse it did. I had to change jobs because the guy I was working for (one of my best friends to this very day) looked me in the eye and said, "I don't have enough work to keep us all busy. You guys need to find something else." I know it was one of the hardest things he ever had to do, but he had to look out for his family. He had already been putting his employees over himself and his family for the last few months. All I could think was, "I'm screwed!"

The next few years would be some of the most humbling and learning years of my life. We didn't lose the house because we decided at that point we had to make a change. Only a few years after we had filed bankruptcy we were in worse shape financially than when we filed before. We had literally hit ROCK BOTTOM. At this point, we had two kids and I felt like a failure as a husband, father, and provider.

So, as I found myself at rock bottom I decided to go to real estate school and see if I could make it in sales. I really couldn't have picked a worse time to get into real estate, but I figured I would give it a try. My wife and I started selling everything that wasn't attached to the walls or floors just to pay the bills. We sold her car, my tools, and a gun collection, anything of value.

I then decided to deliver a paper route in Cincinnati in order to pay the bills as I was trying to get started in real estate. The next, almost two years of my life, were pure hell when it came to finances. I made $16,300 the first year (the least amount of money I ever made as an adult) and was doing every side job and selling anything I could just to stay afloat.

Finally, after a couple years, I started to make a few sales in real estate. My wife had gotten a job at the hospital in our town and we were slowly digging ourselves out of the hole that we had created. Both of us at this time were working fulltime and both of us going fulltime to college. We were also trying to raise the two girls we had at this point and just trying to make ends meet. My wife was also pregnant with our third little girl during this time which made it even harder.

A Second New Beginning

Our story ended up paying off as my wife became one of the best Registered Nurses around and I eventually, after hard work and dedication, opened up my own real estate brokerage. But none of this happened by luck or chance. Nothing happened differently for us until we made a conscious decision to change our way of life. We were the only ones who had the availability to control our outcome of failure or success. And until we realized that, we were broke.

I remember years later my younger brother (probably twenty-five at the time) called me up and asked me if he should file bankruptcy. He had talked with a few other family members and they had all told him yes and said to him bankruptcy was the only way out.

So, I asked him his situation and, not to go in great detail, he told me he owed (from my recollection) somewhere around $7,000 on a car that he had totaled and didn't have gap insurance. I could see me all over again. He had decent credit and a small amount of debt and was being told to take the easy way out. I gave him the best advice I could have at the time. I said no way. I told him my story and helped him understand that $7,000 was nothing in the grand scheme of life and to buckle down and pay it off.

About a year and a half later, he called me up to let me know he had paid the last payment on the $7,000 and no longer had that loan over his head. At this current time in his life, he and his wife have both gone to college and as of last week, he told me have made the last payment on their student loans. They are now debt free! I couldn't be happier for them.

Why Can't We Just Be Content?

One of the biggest lessons I had to learn was being content with what I have. I truly believe being content is one of the hardest things any human will ever have to face in this life. We always seem to want more. We always want the newer, shinier, prettier, better widget. Think about it. How many people do you know right now that are willing to buy a new car (on payments) every couple of years? Or how many of your friends have a $1000 cell phone that they finance for $30 a month. They do all this just to have the newest thing on the market. This is how broke people live. Some of the wealthiest people I know or have ever met have been driving the same vehicle for years and have three or even five-year-old cell phones. Stuff is not as important to them. They have decided to be content.

Notice I said they *decided* to be content. I use that word on purpose because I truly believe contentment is a choice we have to make. I remember this older (very successful) gentleman that I worked with when I first got into real estate. He gave me a lesson on contentment one day that I will never forget. I was telling him how I was going to buy this new truck and all the stuff I wanted to buy and how I switched vehicles every year or sometimes sooner.

He looked me dead in the eye and said: "Son, you are never going to be successful with an attitude like that." I looked with a blank stare in disbelief. He went on to say, "Until you can find contentment and be happy with what you have today, you will never be able to be successful in life." I couldn't believe he had just said that to me. This was a man I respected a lot and he just rained on my parade.

What I ended up realizing is that this was one of the life lessons that helped sculpt me into who I am today. I had never had anyone say anything that bluntly to me before about money or the way I visualized "stuff." My thoughts on things like this had never been challenged.

Every other time when I talked about buying this or buying that, everyone else just agreed with me. They thought it was a great idea. And now this guy, a guy I really admired, called me out on it.

Contentment Is a Choice

After years of destroying my finances multiple times and putting my family into financial ruin, I finally realized "stuff" does not make us happy. Stuff is just something to make others think you are happy. Most of the "stuff" we buy is for other people anyway and not even for us. We buy it to look good for them or show them how great we are doing. We want them to see how much better we have it than they do. And until we change that mindset, we simply can't be financially free.

I had a lot of bad routines that I had taught myself over the years. Some were passed down from the family and some were self-taught. Either way, they were horrible routines. I had taught myself how important "stuff" was to me and that I was willing to do whatever it took and sacrifice whatever I needed to in order to get it. I would spend no matter what and no one was going to hold me back. I was willing to destroy my family and my finances for "stuff."

I know this last chapter has been quite a glimpse into some of my own experiences and how I got to where I am today, but I just want you to understand how messed up our thought process can be. I mean, I literally had to forget everything I was ever taught about money and how to handle it before I could ever be successful.

And I would say for most of you, it's going to be the same. You are going to have to forget everything you were taught about money and begin making new habits and new routines. Instead of watching three or four hours of TV every night, read a book. Read an article about finances. Have a conversation with someone who has done it, someone who thinks differently than you do. One of my favorite quotes is from one the professors I had in college. He would always say "if there are three of us in the room and we all agree, then there are two too many people."

What he was saying is seek out people who think differently than you do. Find people who will challenge your thoughts. A successful person is willing to admit they are wrong and they don't feel intimidated by someone who has a different opinion than them. Remember the definition I gave you earlier. Insanity is doing the same thing over and over again and expecting different results. Change your mindset and you will change your future.

CHAPTER 3
YOU ARE NEVER TOO BROKE TO START

The funny thing is I have had so many people come up to me and say how lucky I am or how easy it was for me to start my own company. When they see me with my rental properties or flipping houses they always say, "it must be nice!" I mean really!! They have no idea what it took me to get to this point in my life. I worked my ass off for years to do this and "easy" never came to mind.

I started out broke, and made myself more broke by my own stupid financial decisions. I even delivered a paper route in the middle of the night in downtown Cincinnati just to make ends meet. There was nothing easy about anything I did. I simply did not give up.

My one buddy, who also owns his own business, and me have joked about this exact thing. We call it the overnight success that took ten years to create. No one wants to focus on the work it took to get to the point of where a successful business person is; rather they only focus on them once they've arrived at the point of success.

Winning Is a Conscious Decision

Now, I truly believe that if you want something in life you can obtain it. Now does that mean it's going to be easy or just fall into your lap? Hell, no! It means you need to get off your ass and do something about it. Nothing in this world is free and no one is going to give you something for nothing.

But winning is a mindset. Unfortunately, most people will never choose to win. Most people will continue living their lives just as they always have. They will never do anything different and complain that the outcome never changes. They will tell everyone how horrible they have had it and complain about all the people that have it so much better than they do. They will tell everyone how hard life is and all they need is a "lucky break." They are the same people who never take responsibility for their own actions and always blame others. These are the types of people I will not associate with for very long.

In order to win in life, you have to first want to win. That means you have to get up every single day trying to figure out how to win. It means at night you are constantly thinking of new ideas and trying to figure out new ways to do things. If you sit at home every evening and watch TV for four hours and wonder why your brain is rotting away, here's your sign! Wake up!

The only person who can change your outcome is you. No one is going to do it for you. You have to make a conscious decision every single day to do better. You have to wake up wanting more than you had the day before. Because trust me, on the other side of town, on the other side of the state, there is a guy or a girl who wants it worse than you do. They are not sleeping, they are not watching TV or browsing social media, but rather they are trying to figure out how to create the next social media site. These types of people have chosen to win. And with that sort of attitude, they most definitely will.

You Can Start with Nothing

I also love it when people tell me that they don't have any money, so they can't do it. Well, guess what. Eleven years ago, I was flat broke making $16,300 a year and now I own my own real estate business, have multiple rentals paid for, have no personal debt and flip four or five houses a year. And I started with nothing. I mean *absolutely* nothing!

The thing I learned early on was if you don't have any money to start, then you have to sell yourself. You have to convince people that YOU bring something to the table, something that they can use, something that makes you useful to them. That is exactly what I did. When I started in real estate I was broke and had literally no credit. So, I decided I needed to sell me. I needed to show people that I did have value and that I did have something to bring to the table.

After being in real estate for about a year or a little longer, I started building relationships with other real estate agents, brokers, and investors. I remember some of them talking about thousands of dollars like it was nothing, while I was trying to figure out how I could afford a burger and fries at the nearest burger joint when I went out to lunch with them. But these guys were winners. These guys decided they were going to do what it took to win.

I finally became very close to this group of guys who were investors and I would help them a lot of times for free; do things on some of the houses they flipped or the rentals they had. I would show them that I had value. Remember, I used to be a plumber a few years back, so I still had that skill. And trust me, in rentals and house flipping, that is a very good skill to have. Also, I could do a lot of other construction type jobs simply because I had been in that field.

After doing a lot of work for free and showing them what value I had, one of them asked me if I would ever want to join their investment group and buy a house to flip with them. I remember chuckling and saying, "that would be great, but I have literally no money or credit." I remember the one investor (who eventually became one of my best friends) saying no worries. We will buy them, and you can just help us fix the plumbing and a few things.

I was so ecstatic I could hardly contain myself. These guys that knew I had nothing were willing to take me under their wings just because of who I was. They bought me. They knew I didn't have any money or any credit and they still took me on. To this day, I am thankful for each and every one of them.

After a while, we were flipping a few houses a year. And eventually, I didn't do the plumbing anymore. We just ended up hiring it out. I then began to run the business account and learn that side of it. That is where I got a first glimpse of how money can work for you if you let it.

I remember the first big check I received. I got a check for $15,000 which was my share of the sale of a couple houses we had sold. And at that time in my life, $15,000 was like a million dollars to me. I mean, just a couple years ago that was about all I made in a year. I was so excited. I had been doing a lot of reading and didn't just want to waste this opportunity. I wanted to make this money count. Now remember, this was in the Great Recession, so houses were still dirt cheap at this point. So, I decided I would look around for a cheap house to buy and fix up as a rental. And that is exactly what I did.

I found my first rental for $13,000. With the other $2,000 and my skills, I fixed the house up and only had a little over $15,000 in it. I rented that home for $500 a month for seven years before I sold it. At that point in my life that was not much more than my house payment. So basically, I had someone else paying my house payment. Since I didn't have a mortgage on the rental house it was nearly all profit to me. That was one of the best decisions I ever made and was the first decision I ever made where my money actually was working for me.

Timing Is Everything

If I would have had the same amount of money just a year or two earlier, there is no doubt in my mind I would have spent it on something stupid. Like a boat, truck, car, motorcycle, etc. that would have continually cost me more money.

But this time something was different. This time I was remembering the words of the Old Guy that worked a couple offices down from me. "You'll never be successful until you are content with what you have today." So, I chose to be content with what I had and used the money to invest it and make me more money.

And because of that choice, I now had a house paid for free and clear that ended up making me $45,000 over the time I had it, plus my initial investment back. If I would have just spent that money on "stuff" it would have been gone to never return again.

"NO" Means Try Harder

I said earlier how my and my wife's interest rate on our house was crazy high and it was an interest-only mortgage. Well as I said before, the first time I went to the bank to try and refinance our mortgage the banker said NO! He didn't think about it, he didn't talk about it, he simply said NO.

We even tried going to my wife's grandmother, who was a loan officer at a local bank, and even her answer was NO. This NO word was becoming too familiar to me. It was almost becoming like second nature. It was like I already knew the answer from the bank before I even picked up the phone and dialed.

After hearing it over and over I decided again I had to make a choice. I could listen to the word NO and take it for what it means on the surface, or in my mind, I had another definition of the word. I convinced myself that the word NO simply meant I wasn't trying hard enough. (I know my mind works a little differently than most people.)

Now, I don't mean I needed to go to more banks or keep begging at the ones I had already asked. No, by trying harder, I mean I needed to change. Just as I had shown the group of investors that I had a skill that was useful in flipping houses; I needed to show the bankers that I could do this as well. I needed to give them a reason to believe in me. I needed to sell myself.

So that is exactly what I did. First thing I did was called my current mortgage company and negotiated more time on my current variable rate before the rate went up. My current rate was about to expire and without re-negotiating my payment would have almost doubled. Our current interest rate of 7.9% was set to go up 5% to 12.9%. I knew if that happened we would be facing foreclosure. But I was not giving up. I had worked this hard and gotten this far so I was bound and determined to make it through this somehow.

I pleaded with the mortgage company to give us another year before the rate would rise, causing our payment to go up. After many long conversations and giving them all sorts of paperwork to show them we had made nothing the past couple years, they finally agreed.

After that, I knew my next step was to convince a local bank to take a chance on me and help me refinance the home. I finally got one of the lenders at a local bank to give me the time of day. This was a lender that I had met through selling real estate. So maybe at first, he just met me and my wife to appease me. However, after talking to us and listening to our situation and our story, he decided to give us a chance.

I am forever grateful for him taking a chance on us. We were able to refinance the home and get a fixed rate at 5.5% which was lower than the interest only rate we currently had. We were so happy because for the first time in a few years, we were actually paying on the principle of our home.

Being told *No* so many times really taught me a few things. We have to be willing to show others our value. We have to be willing to stand up for what we believe and let people know our worth. But in order to do it, you have to change. People can see through a fake person. If I had not changed my mindset from years prior and would have tried to refinance my house, it would have never happened. They would have seen through me like a screen door.

But once the lender heard my story and realized the changes I had made since my own financial self-destruction, he was willing to take a shot. People will see the real you, so you better make sure the real you is someone you are willing to expose. Anyone of us can do this. But it will ultimately be us who decides whether we choose to win or lose.

CHAPTER 4
WHY NOT DOING THE "NORM" MAKES YOU STAND OUT

I really do believe that going against the norm of society is a very large key factor in financial freedom. I believe that if we try and continue to live like everyone else, financial freedom is almost unattainable. But the funny thing is, once you begin going against the norm of what everyone else does, then the financial part just seems to come automatically.

Think about when I took the $15,000 (basically the only money I had) and bought a house with it. I had people tell me I was crazy. I had people say I should have bought all this other materialistic "stuff." I had people asking me if I knew we were in a recession and houses were going to nothing. But I didn't listen to any of them. I knew that the house had a value. And yes, that value was lower the day I bought it due to a recession, but it would eventually go back up.

I also knew that instead of spending money on something that would cost me more money or take my money away; I had spent it on something that made me money on a monthly basis. And quite honestly, pretty damn good money. I mean I had a $15,000 investment that was soon making me $6000 a year. That is a 40% return. Most investors would kill for that sort of a return.

I bought when everyone else was freaking out. I went against the norm of society and did what most would not. I remember Warren Buffett (who many people would say is the greatest investor of all time) said, "Buy when everyone else is selling." He is basically saying when people are selling because of panic, that's the time to get in. So that's what I did. I chose to buy a house when almost no one else would even consider touching real estate. Another one of Buffett's famous quotes is, "The stock market is a device for transferring money from the impatient to the patient."

The mindset is the same here. Most people want instant gratification and have no patience to wait. I could have taken that $15,000 and had a heck of a time, buying whatever. But I chose a smarter path. I chose to buy something that would continue to make me money for years to come. Something that showed the banks I am different. I had to show them that I went outside of the norm and did something that most people would never do.

No One Wants To Change, but Rather Complain

Well, hopefully, there are still a few people left reading this book at this point. I'm sure by now I've most definitely lost some if not most. Most people have no interest in changing their habits. They would rather sit back and complain about everyone else and how much better the other person has it then they have it. Well if that's you, listen carefully. Put this book down, go back to the couch with a bag of Cheetos® and turn the next reality TV show on so your brain can continue rotting with lies.

The truth is, it's hard to change and sometimes really hard. We have an entire society telling us to do one thing and a few other people saying something different. We literally have to go against the grain of society. We have to do what no one else is doing and look like the oddball. It's one thing to read a book or talk about changing the way we think financially but wait until you actually do it. Wait until you buy that first investment that gives you a return like a house, or a stock or whatever, and everyone looks at you like you are crazy.

I remember when my wife and I bought that first rental. We were so proud. We had done something no one on either side of our families had ever done. We had bought an investment instead of blowing our money on something stupid and useless. I will never forget talking to some of our family about what we had done and how we had done it. I wasn't trying to brag but was just so super excited and wanted to let people know that they could do something like this as well. I remember some of them seeming to have interest, but others saying things like, "once you're a millionaire can I have some."

Of course, at that time I laughed it off. But looking back I wish I would have said no. Get off your ass and I'll show you how you can do it too. Why should I work hard while you choose not to and then I just give you some of what I have? But again, hindsight is always 20/20.

Going Against the Grain Is Always Uncomfortable

The unfortunate thing is going against the grain of society really never gets easier. You eventually have to make peace in just knowing that you are different. You have to let a lot of people's cheap comments go by, otherwise you will drive yourself crazy. People who are not like you will not understand the way you think; they can't. They cannot "get it" unless they are doing the same thing. I have talked to people until I was blue in the face about this stuff and they seem like they get it, just to go off the next day or so and make some impulsive, stupid purchase.

The best part is when they come back and start to try and justify it to you like you are the financial police. I don't give two shits what you do with your money. After all, it is your money. If you want to die broke, that is up to you. This book is for people who want to make a change with their finances and hear from someone that did it.

The further in life you go (as long as you continue making good financial decisions) the better off you'll be. You can begin to acquire assets, build net worth and savings. The more you make your money work for you, the more free time you will have. This will allow you to do all sorts of things that you wouldn't be able to if you had a massive amount of debt. But don't think that just because you have more free time (because of your good decisions) that people will be happy for you. A lot of them will be jealous, try to take your time and even make fun of you for having more free time than they do.

I remember a couple years ago I was at an amusement park in Cincinnati with my wife and kids. The past few years my wife and I have done pretty well. We are in the top 5% earners in our area and we have a lot more free time than most people. But again, that's because we changed our mindset and even went without things to be able to do what we do.

But I digress. At that time in my life, I was really involved in this church organization. I was volunteering weekly and was going to meetings often. But that day I got a text because I had missed a meeting to take the kids to the amusement park. Granted I had told them prior I would not be at the meeting, but that wasn't good enough.

Next thing I know I'm getting made fun of because I am spending time with my family. I don't know if it was because none of them could do it with their families or what the deal was, all I know is it clearly was something they didn't like. I heard things like "slacker," "it must be nice," "I guess not all of us have to work all the time," and so on. It was really aggravating simply because it shows how childish people can get when you are different than them. Simply put, people do not like you being different than the norm and if you are, they will call you out.

My wife and I also like to take a few trips a year. And, we have worked to be able to do it. We both work extremely hard for our money and have made a number of sacrifices to get to where we are today.

But don't be naïve in thinking people will congratulate you on your next trip. People will hate it. They will talk about it when you are not around. They will ridicule you and try to make you feel like you are doing something wrong. And I even mean good people. Your family, people at work, people at your church or religious organizations, your friends, almost everyone.

The bad thing is, they are trained in their heads to think like this and don't even realize it. It's almost like it's not even their fault. They are taught as young kids that we must do the same thing everyone else does. That we just go to school, go to college, get a job, take a week or so off a year, live in debt, payoff your mortgage at sixty five or seventy, retire and die.

I'm sorry to say, but I don't agree with that at all. I believe we all have choices to make every day. I believe we can be whoever we want to be and have whatever job we would like. College is important, but don't let anyone tell you it's a necessity. There is smart college and dumb college. There are things that make sense and things that do not.

To give you a prime example, my wife, Felicity, is a registered nurse. She must have a degree to work in that field. However, she did it the smart way. She got her associate degree and took her RN test and began work. A few years later she went back and got her bachelor's degree and we were able to pay it off the year she graduated.

We have to get out of this mindset that the world and our society wants us to buy into. Just look around. Did you know that in 2017 the majority of people in the US (57%) have less than $1,000 in their savings account? That is just mind-boggling to me. It isn't a wonder that the average household credit card debt is over $15,000 right now. That is a life I have no interest in living anymore. And these are the same people who make fun of you or me for doing things differently.

I wish our society would wake up. We put so much value on "stuff" that we are willing to risk everything we have to get it. And we put no value on our time. We are fine having less than $1,000 in our savings and owing an average of $15,000 on credit cards, an average of $172,000 on mortgages, an average of $28,000 in vehicle loans and almost $50,000 in student loans. This is crazy! This is what we are teaching our kids in school. This is what we, as parents, are telling our kid is all right. Something has got to change.

Don't Be Fake

When did we get to a point when we would rather look like we are successful than actually be successful? Think how crazy that is! We want people to think we have money, but most of us do not. The problem is we would rather spend tomorrow's money and have no problem at all borrowing to do it. We just act like nothing will ever change in our life or our jobs and that things will be exactly like they are right now *forever*. It's actually scary to think that people are so brainwashed into believing this way.

The only way to change any of this is to change our mindsets. And it has to start with us and our kids. We have got to do things differently and help our kids see that "stuff" is not important. We need to teach them that our time is way more valuable than any possession could ever be. We have got to start teaching them about money, what it is and how to make it work for them. We need to teach them the importance of not having debt and not spending tomorrow's money just to have the newest "stuff" to impress everyone. No one is going to teach any of this to your kids and unfortunately, most adults will never even listen to these points themselves.

The ideology that successful people should be made fun of or that they don't deserve it has got to stop. Instead of ridiculing people who have more time than you or are more financially successful than you, why don't you ask them how they have accomplished it? Why don't you ask to buy them a cup of coffee and pick their brain?

Most successful people would love to help you understand how they got to where they are in life. A lot of them started out just like me or you and love to tell their story. Instead, we continue to make fun of them and belittle them. Instead, we chose to go down the same paths and continue the same patterns that we always have and wonder why nothing is different. We have got to get in the habit of not living like the typical person in America. We need to congratulate people on their success stories and not ridicule them.

The unfortunate thing is even most of our schools don't get it. They go on teaching whatever curriculum the state has deemed worthy and never question it. And even though our debt as a nation and as individuals is as high as it's ever been, we continue the same processes we always have. We have got to make a change and we cannot fear standing out.

Being normal in this society makes you broke. Doing things differently than the normal will make you wealthy. We have got to quit complaining, get off our asses and change our mindset.

CHAPTER 5
ALL DEBT IS NOT BAD DEBT

I listen to a lot of talk radio. I find it very informative. Besides, listening to the same songs' playing over and over on other conventional FM stations just simply bores me. I would rather listen to someone give me a new idea or tell me a story about something they are doing and have done then listen to the newest boy band or teen pop icon.

The other day as I was listening to the radio, one of the financial folks from a nearby firm came on. Instantly I connect with her thought process. It's about Christmas time so she was talking about gift giving and if it makes sense. She starts going through the idea of just having an experience at Christmas instead of exchanging $25 gifts that no one really wants or cares about anyway.

I actually thought the idea was genius, and I am going to even try to begin implementing it in our family. Her idea was this: Instead of each family member—brother, sister, Mom and Dad—giving presents, why not go out and have a nice dinner together? Or maybe go catch that movie you've all been dying to see?

Honestly, the possibilities are endless. There are so many things that we could do as an "experience" rather than give each other hand towels or a shirt that doesn't fit. I believe wholeheartedly in giving, but why not give *you* in conversation vs a crappy gift.

I know some of you right now are thinking I've lost my mind, but to me, it makes the most sense. I believe that time is the most valuable asset we have in this life and to me; if you give it to someone it is the greatest gift you can give. So why not give a little of it towards your family and show them that you really do appreciate them?

Now don't get me wrong. I'm not talking about giving a nine-year-old a dinner and a movie for Christmas. I'm talking about adults and even later teens. If I tried to give my nine-year-old daughter a dinner and a movie under the tree I'm not sure who I would have to fight first, her or my wife!

I'm just saying we waste so much money and even time trying to find a crappy gift that we don't want to buy in the first place and quite honestly a gift most people could care less about getting. Then everyone has to do the "fake" thank you, it's so great, I love it. I have an idea! Let's cut all the bullshit and just spend time with each other.

You know it's funny, because for the longest time, even as a teenager Thanksgiving has always been my favorite holiday. No, it's not because I don't believe in Christmas, but it's because of what Christmas has become. Thanksgiving is now getting that way with black Friday and sales on Thanksgiving Day etc., but for the longest time, it was simple. It was about getting together with family and friends and just simply being happy and thankful for what you have today. Not worrying about what you can buy tomorrow (that is starting to change now), but rather just taking it easy with an experience. To me, this is what Christmas should be about as well. Not all this commercialized crap we've made it.

You may wonder why I brought up Christmas, presents, and spending, but believe it or not there is a point to this. One of the other things the lady on the talk radio show said was this. The average American still owes $600 from last year's Christmas on their current credit card. They still have not fully paid off all they bought the year before. Are you kidding me?

I'll be honest, even that one threw me for a loop. It just boggles my mind how people can be so stupid with money. Don't get me wrong. I did the same thing years ago and was maybe even the king of it, but I can't believe I was that stupid either. I just wish that I could walk around to each person that does something like this and smack them on the head and say, "Wake UP Stupid!" I guess I could, but I would probably have to fight a lot.

I mean, think about the consequences of that. If you owe $600 from last year and you are just paying the minimum payment you are barely making headway. I mean it's almost compound interest in reverse. (We will get to compound interest later on in the book.) Then we get into this year, (if they can't pay for last year) they are going to add an additional $600 if not more to it. Now your payment is twice as much and so is your debt. Unless something changes, this is a cycle that will never end until you are bankrupt.

I just hate when I see people spend tomorrow's money for today's satisfaction. It just simply doesn't make sense. We have lost all patience in this world and in our personal lives. We want this instant gratification, and everything must be done right now. We are not willing to buy our kids one or two gifts; instead, we buy them fifteen or twenty and wonder if that is enough. Really!

Is this what Christmas is all about? Is this what we want to teach our children? Maybe we all need to sit down and watch the Charlie Brown Christmas Special again and take a lesson from Linus. Today Christmas is commercialized at its best and we have almost all bought into it.

Blowing money like this is horrible debt. Honestly the worst kind. We are buying things that we don't need and even worse, for the most part, don't even want. It's just impulsive buying. Why do you think that Wal-Mart, Kroger, or Lowes put things in the middle of the aisles? Why do you think when you pull up Amazon one of the first things you see is "deals of the day?"

They are not doing this to try and help you out or make life convenient for you. They are doing this for the impulse buyer. They know that statistics have proven, the majority of people will walk by or browse by and see a sign that says "deal" and next thing you know, they must have it. They are playing tricks on your mind and we are all falling for it.

It never ceases to amaze me how people are willing to destroy their families, themselves and their lives simply to buy "stuff." We are so addicted to "stuff" that we will get it at any cost. We will lie, cheat, borrow, and steal to get what we think we want. And I mean really good people. The only people that are immune to such things are people who choose to be, people who make a conscious decision to not get caught up in the antics.

I mean, think about it. We borrow to buy our house, we borrow to buy our vehicles, we borrow to buy our clothes, we borrow to buy our jewelry, we borrow to buy our entertainment, we borrow to buy our vacations, and sometimes we even borrow to buy our food! It's not a wonder that the average credit card debt is almost $15,000. Credit card companies love us. Car dealers love us!

Everyone thinks they've accomplished something because they can get a loan and borrow money. Well, trust me, that is no accomplishment. At best it's an impatient way to get stuff and at its worst it's a tool for financial self-destruction. I would lean towards the latter.

Good Debt vs. Bad Debt

Now I know some of you are thinking right now that I've lost it. I mean I just said how bad I hate debt and that I think it can be a tool for self-destruction. And yes, I not only believe this, but I've seen it happen. My buddy's wife went back to college to get a master's degree in counseling and spent $85,000 to do it. And I don't mean she wrote a check. I mean she borrowed $85,000 worth of student loans.

Think about how crazy that is. $85,000 at 6% interest for a thirty-year period is $509 a month. I mean, that's almost another house payment. It would maybe make a little more sense if you could make at least $85,000 a year in our area doing it, but unfortunately, you can't.

In this area, you will make around $30,000-$34,000 on a good day. So, after taxes (assuming a 25% tax bracket) you bring home around $2100 a month. Take out the $500 for the student loan payment and now you're down to $1600. You break that down to 160 hours a month (forty hours a week) and you are bringing home around $10 an hour. I mean minimum wage is almost that and, in some states, it is actually higher than that.

No, I'm not saying college is bad and student loan debt never makes sense. But the math has to work. I have another buddy. He and his wife are both Doctors of Theology. They borrowed around $100,000 together, but they made some great decisions. They work at a university; where they have free housing (as part of their salary,) almost no bills and make somewhere over $50,000 each a year.

The last time I spoke with him, they had their student loans almost completely paid for just about four years after graduating. This is how you make sense of student debt. You have to treat it like any other debt. The thirty-year plan will simply not work. There are a number of debts I would call good debt. I think a student loan can be one if it is used right. But again "IF" becomes a key factor, as it does in most debts.

I have no problem with a mortgage if it's used right. I believe wholeheartedly in a maximum fifteen-year mortgage. If you can't pull that off you either rent until you can, or you buy something cheaper. It's really that simple. The problem again is we have no patience. We want the same size or style of house that our parents live in and have worked their entire lives to buy. Or we want the newer house and convince ourselves it's worth it because there are fewer repairs. Well, I'm here to tell you to buy what you can afford.

It took our parents thirty to forty years to be able to accumulate the "stuff" they have. We can't expect to get out of high school or college and have everything they worked their entire lives for. Oh wait, that's exactly what we are taught; instant gratification. Patience is gone by the wayside.

Another debt I don't mind and actually would even be really okay with is a mortgage on a rental property. Now on rental properties, my numbers are a little different. You do not borrow for more than ten years for a rental and if you can't afford it, then again you don't buy it.

I had a great friend of mine (one of my former professors) who, after he passed away, his wife lost all their rentals. It was not because he was bad with money for the most part. The problem was he bought rentals at the top of the real estate market and passed away during the housing crisis. And he bought all of them with a mortgage. By the time he had passed, his wife could no longer manage or afford to keep them up and she was upside down on all the properties, so she couldn't even sell them. Unfortunately, she ended up losing all of them.

My point is this. If you are going to borrow money for anything it has to make good mathematical sense. I really don't believe in borrowing money at all unless it somehow can make me money in return. And it's not always simple. I'm sure when my former professor bought his rentals, the math made sense to him. Unfortunately, it proved to be a bad investment for him as his debt was bigger than his net worth.

I would also say to never have any business debt more than your net worth. What that means is if you had to sell everything you own, you could pay any outstanding debts or loans you have. This would have saved my professor's wife if she could have just sold the rental properties and paid the notes off. But, unfortunately for her, that was not the case. The debts for the rental properties far exceeded what the value was.

You will never hear me say that a vehicle loan is a good idea. And when I say never, I really mean NEVER!

As a matter of fact, I think it is one of the worst loans available. Car companies love vehicle debt. I mean, think about it. If it weren't for lenders doing loans on these vehicles, most people would never even dream of buying a brand-new car. Car companies would be in a different line of work or their car prices would drop dramatically. As a matter of fact, we would probably all drive the one we had until it wouldn't move anymore.

Nowadays it's just so easy to get a vehicle loan. We just go to the dealership, take the car we just bought a year or two ago (because you know, a two-year-old car is a piece of shit) and trade it in for a newer, better car. Oh, and don't forget the negative equity we roll right into the new vehicle loan. Most of the time we don't even ask or care what the price is; we simply want to know what the payment will be, and we sign on the dotted line. There is no way it's a bad deal, right?

Just a month or so ago I was with one of my good friends and we were in my truck. (My truck is five years old.) He asked me when I was going to trade this old thing in. He said, "it has 80,000 miles, now it's about time for stuff to start breaking." I just kind of chuckled and said, "No, I'm good." I don't believe in just buying a new truck because I can afford to. It still has to make more sense than that to me.

There was a time in my life (not so long ago) when I would have loved to drive something with 80,000 miles. At that point, I would have considered it brand new. We get spoiled. And unfortunately, we do it to ourselves most of the time.

This same friend who asked me this question had just bought himself a new truck last year. His new truck had a price tag of $65,000! That just blows me away. I've bought many houses a lot cheaper than that amount and here we are today spending that sort of money on a truck or a car. The crazy thing is, the truck he traded in was only four years old and he still owed $11,000 on it.

It simply goes back to that instant gratification and never being satisfied or content. We always want more, we always want newer and we always want what everyone else has. Even worse we want to "one-up" what everyone else has. This mindset has got to change. We have got to be content or we will never be successful.

Why Most of Us Don't Even Have $1,000

It's really not a wonder that most people don't even have $1,000 in their savings accounts. We don't save because we don't think it matters. We finance everything we have and then pay the payments. We create this mindset that we will always be in debt and that it's what everyone else does; so it must be okay. We have so many debt payments we cannot even imagine beginning to save. I mean it's normal, right?

The problem is we are a stressed-out nation, depression is ramping higher and higher. We are unhealthy and over 50% of marriages are ending in divorce, but we keep buying "stuff" to fill the void. It's actually insane. Life could be so much less stressful and be fulfilling if we would just change our thought processes. Being normal is not okay. I would love to see it get to the point where NOT being "normal" is being normal. Like when most people begin to save and put away for the future. A life where we are content with what we have today and aren't always trying to buy something better or nicer than our neighbors, our family or our friends.

Can you imagine a life where Facebook is full of experiences that we've had instead of things that we bought? Or imagine a life where holidays become more about family and experiences and not about the "stuff" that we bought.

That's the life I want to live, that's the life I want to raise my kids to live and that's the life I wish every person could see. Until we are "not normal" and do things differently, we will never even be able to get to the $1,000 savings, that most Americans do not have and unfortunately never will.

It's Not My Fault

One of the greatest things I love to hear (I'm saying sarcastically) is when we start blaming others for our bad debt decisions. You know, when we say it's not my fault; like we had no say in it. Like someone at the car dealership held a gun to your head and made you sign to buy that new car when the one you had was perfectly fine. Or like someone made you spend $1,000 at Christmas that you didn't have on your credit card. It's never their fault, but always someone else's. That type of person just goes through me like a dull spoon.

We will never be financially successful or successful in life for that matter until we begin taking responsibility for our own actions. It's my fault I filed bankruptcy. Mine and mine alone. Not my mom, not my dad and not even my wife. It was mine. I'm the one who made the bad decisions, made impulsive purchases and signed up for every loan or credit card I could get. I did that.

We have to be able to look ourselves in the mirror and say, "hey stupid, you screwed up, but you can change this, and you can fix this." Until we are brave enough to do that, then we will not succeed financially.

Some of the most financially successful people in the world have failed. You know the difference between them and most people? They take responsibility and they learn from their failures. They choose to study and analyze the failure and see what went wrong. They want to know when they made the bad decision, why they made the decision, and how they can change it the next time.

Winning is a conscious decision. It doesn't happen by accident, it happens on purpose and by choice. Warren Buffett didn't become the greatest investor of all time by accident. He had a purpose. And when he failed, he changed to make it better the next time. Michael Jordan didn't become the greatest basketball player of all time by sitting on the couch and just showing up at the games. He chose to practice like no one else did.

The only one that can control how successful we are in life is us. We have a choice to make. It's up to us what we do with our time, with our money, with our success, and with our failures. You have to get it in your head that giving up is not even an option. Making bad debt decisions does not predetermine your life and what or who you will become. That decision is on you.

Making bad debt decisions is a tool (if you allow it to be) that you can learn from. It is a tool that you can use for the rest of your life.

One of my good friends told me once that a bad financial decision was like paying tuition to go to school. If you spend $1,000 on a credit card on an impulsive buy, then you spent $1,000 on a lesson in financial management.

It's up to you what you do with the lesson. You can learn from it or you can do nothing with it. No different than someone paying for a degree. They can use it in their life or they can throw It in the trash and choose a whole different career.

Winning is a choice. I think Vince Lombardi said it best when he said, "winners never quit, and quitters never win, and that perfection is not attainable, but if we chase perfection we can catch excellence."

CHAPTER 6
ASSETS AND LIABILITIES

What Qualifies as an Asset?

A lot of people have no idea what an asset is. I have heard many people say their home is an asset or their car is an asset. I've even heard people say things like boats, motorcycles and ATV's are assets. Well, not to burst your bubble, but most of these in your life, if not all of them, are probably not assets at all to you.

An asset is something that you own of value. First of all, you must own it, not owe on it! I would like to go a step further and say it's something that you own of value that makes you money. And yes, being worth something could ultimately make you money if you sold that asset.

The problem is most people owe on all of this stuff. Most people in the United States owe on their homes for most of their lives, owe on their vehicles and whatever other toys they decided to buy. If you don't owe on any of it, then all of them could be considered assets.

But let's take your house for instance. If your house is worth $200,000 and you owe $175,000 on it, you really can't consider it an asset. You may be thinking "Wait. I have $25,000 equity, so at least $25,000 should be considered an asset, right?"

I would say "wrong." If you decided to sell your home, you are going to have fees involved to do so. It's going to cost you on average around 10% to sell your home with real estate commissions; seller paid closing costs, home inspection repairs and attorney fees. Not to mention the transfer taxes and property taxes you'll have to pay. So, your $25,000 equity just became almost obsolete and you will basically break even.

Most people don't consider this, but you have to think about all of this when you're trying to figure out if something is or should be considered an asset to you.

Now if your home is paid for it is an asset. Even though you will have the same fees to sell it, you now have a significant amount of equity and it creates a larger amount of net worth. And if you were to ever rent your home, then it becomes not only an asset but a tool to make your money grow even more for you.

Take a rental home, for example. Rental homes are almost always considered an asset even if you owe on them. The reason being this; if you have a rental property someone else is paying you to live there. It is almost always the case that the tenant is paying you more than your mortgage payment (if you have one).

So, for instance, if you owe $30,000 on a ten-year note and your payment is $300 a month, then typically the tenant will be paying you around $700 plus a month to live there. So even after taxes, insurance and maintenance, you are not only making money every month, you also have someone else paying your debt. This is great because someone else is creating your wealth.

I am a strong believer in having all your debts paid for; personal and business as quickly as possible. A personal debt I am almost totally against with the exception of a fifteen-year mortgage, but even business debt can be a hindrance. Even though I design my business debt to be paid for by that business (rentals, business incomes, etc.) I still want it to be gone as soon as it can.

I would rather have the entire value of the asset making me money than a portion. And the quicker it's paid for the quicker that will happen.

Now, when you get into things like cars, trucks, boats, motorcycles and so on, they are almost never an asset for most people and never will be. Remember an asset is something you "own" of value. Now to fully own something, you can't owe anything on it. And unfortunately, most people owe on all of these things for the entirety of owning them and then continue the cycle when they trade them in for newer things.

We discussed in a previous chapter how most people have a vehicle loan. And actually, that number is about 84% of people. Doesn't that seem crazy to think that 84% of people finance something just to drive around in? I mean WOW! When all we really need to do is save for a few months and buy something outright.

There are a few exceptions to every rule, of course. My grandpa, about twenty years ago, bought an old Ford pickup. I think the year of the truck was somewhere in the late 1950's or early 1960's. It was a truck that needed a lot of work. He ended up putting a lot of money into it as well as a lot of time. By the time he was done, you would have never known it was the same pickup. I mean, this thing was immaculate. Everything was new, it was shiny, and it was beautiful.

He ended up taking it to some of the car shows around and even took it to the Cavalcade of Customs in Cincinnati. He didn't win there, but my point is, this was a truck that had value; and furthermore, a truck that could make him money. He took an old truck that was in bad shape that may be worth a thousand or two and made it worth fifty thousand or possibly more.

This was an asset to him, but something like that is rare. Most people have a brand-new truck or car that they owe more than the vehicle is worth. And even if they did put it on the market and sold it, they couldn't even get the payoff.

The next thing is the "toys" of our lives. You know, the boats, motorcycles, ATV's, Jet Skis and so on. These things like vehicles are almost always not an asset. Yes, they have value, but again almost everyone finances these stupid things. If you went out and paid cash, yes, you could consider it an asset. I mean, it will probably never make you any money beyond the value of what it is, and they typically decline in value as soon as they leave the lot. But, if you don't owe on it, then you could call it an asset.

But again, most people don't do that. Most people buy these sorts of things when they are already financially broke.

Most people are trying to fill a void in their lives and they convince themselves that financing a new boat, or a new motorcycle is all they need to be at ease again. Well, guess what? Wrong again!

Buying more crap and creating more debt is in no way, shape or form going to make your life less stress-free or any easier at all. As a matter of fact, it is going to make it suck that much more. The first time you have to pay that payment (especially on something sitting in the garage during the winter) you are going to hate life! You ever heard of buyer's remorse? Well, guess what, it's a real thing and in a situation like I've described, you get to experience it.

I remember a guy I used to work with years ago came into the plumbing shop one day all proud of his newest toy. He had gone out and bought a brand-new boat over the weekend. It was shiny with a beautiful red and silver metallic coat of paint. And of course, it had a nice bright red trailer to pull behind his truck.

It was all anyone could ask for. He worked hard so he deserved it, right?

I remember him telling us that his payment was only $175 a month and that he got it on a ten-year loan. He said he did it that way, so he could afford it. I didn't think like this then, but now I think, "What the HELL!" a ten-year boat payment?

No thanks. I don't want a ten year *any* toy payment. And if I do have a ten-year payment, it better be making me money in some way, shape or form.

Don't I Deserve It?

I think this is one of the biggest problems we face. Not only do people convince us that we deserve this "stuff," but we buy into it. We believe it. And we actually convince ourselves that it's okay to believe. It just goes back to not doing the "norm" that people have created.

Well, I've got news for you. You don't deserve anything. And I mean nothing. Yes, if you work hard you can buy things you want or need, but that doesn't mean you deserve them. It just hurts my head every time I hear someone say the words you deserve it.

Don't get me wrong. I think people (that can afford it) should buy things they want or go to places they would like to see and even splurge a little. But to say we deserve it is taking it a step too far for me. I like to say that I am blessed and that I am grateful for what I have.

I think this mindset is what is lacking in most people today. Most people walk through life ungrateful for everything they do have. They are jealous of everything they don't have, and they think that if you do have something more than them you should share it with them because they "deserve" it too.

The only way you are going to get anything out of this life is to work for it. Quit blaming your bad financial decisions on someone else. Quit saying I wish I had what they had. If you want it that bad, figure out a way to work, save the money and get it. If I see you doing something good in your life, I am going to pick your brain to figure out how you did what you did. No one wants to work anymore. It seems like everyone just wants something for nothing and that has got to change.

I also get tired of this mindset of "I can't work." Bullshit! I knew a local guy once who was paralyzed from a car accident. This guy was offered full-time disability, but when he told the state that he was going to continue his cabinet making business on the side, they told him he could not do it and get his disability. So basically, the state wanted him to just sit around and do nothing or you don't get your disability check.

Guess what? This wasn't going to work for this guy. He chose to waive his disability and continue his business from a wheelchair. And he did a damn good job at it. Again, being successful is a choice!

The Biggest Asset

The biggest asset that any of us will ever have is ourselves. That's right, we are an asset. Have you ever looked at yourself like that? Just think about how much money you can make yourself over a lifetime. Even just working a "regular" job at $50,000 a year for a thirty-year period gives you a lifetime of 1.5 million dollars earned. How many other assets do you have that will give you that kind of return?

Most people just never consider themselves assets. But the truth is you have the availability to go out and earn money. Sometimes that is you working forty hours a week for a company and sometimes it is you owning the company. Either way, you are an asset.

Remember, I like the definition of an asset explained like this: something of value that can give you a return or in a sense make you money. And that is exactly what you are as a human. You have the opportunity to do great things. And the beautiful thing is you don't owe on yourself.

The only one that can screw you up and not allow you to make money is you. Everyone has opportunities to use the gifts they have in some fashion. We all have different talents, skills, dreams, and visions. All this can be used as a tremendous asset if we just get out of our own way.

CHAPTER 7
GOOD EXPENSES VS BAD EXPENSES

Good Expenses?

Everyone that does anything in life will have expenses. Expenses can range anything from fuel in your car to the groceries you need to survive. But you will find that the more successful you become, the more you will need to understand expenses and how they can work for you.

I know right off hand you may be thinking how any expense can be good. Well, let me explain. Say I am the owner of a company. I have ten employees and with these ten employees, I am making a gross profit of one million dollars a year. (A gross income is your money before expenses and a net income is your gross minus all expenses and deductions.).

Now, in order to find out my net, I need to know my expenses. We can start off by figuring what each one of these employees cost me. If each one is making an average of $50,000 a year salary, then I have $500,000 right of the top going to my employee expense. Then say I have an additional $3,000 a month going to a lease or mortgage. I have another $24,000 going to supplies and $10,000 a year in utilities, insurances, and other expenses.

Now we can figure out what my net income would be by simple mathematics. $1,000,000 - $500,000 - $36,000 - $24,000 -$10,000 = $430,000. So, my net income is $430,000. That's pretty good. That is a 43% profit margin.

Now, in order to decide if each expense I have is a good expense or a bad expense, I need to know what it produces.

For example, I know I need a building to run my business in order to provide the service or product that I am selling. So that $36,000 a year is a good expense. The only way it would not be would be if the space I had was too large and/or I could get a similar space cheaper. Now let's use the utilities, phones, internet and other expenses.

Again, in order to produce the products/services my company sells, these are expenses that just come with the territory. These are expenses that I will have just about anywhere I do my business from and therefore, as long as those services are making me money, they are good expenses.

Now let's say nine of my employees are killing it. And let's say that these nine employees out of the ten I have are producing $960,000 of the $1,000,000 that I am grossing. These employees are well worth the money. Mathematically, I am making over $106,000 for each of those nine employees that I am paying $50,000 a year. Not too bad.

Now, what about employee number ten? What's his story? I am paying him the same amount of money as the others ($50,000 a year) and he is only producing $40,000 in gross income. So, he is actually costing me $10,000 a year and that's not including any other expenses I would take out of that.

So even though the company is making money, I would actually be better off getting rid of employee number ten and making $960,000 that next year. By getting rid of employee ten, my gross goes down to $960,000 but my net goes up to $440,000 ($960,000 - $450,000 - $36,000 - $24,000-$10,000= $440,000) which actually raised my profit margin to 44% vs 43%.

Just because you make more money on a gross number, it doesn't always translate into a better net number. In this scenario, I was doing fine with the ten employees and even making good money. But one of them was not pulling their weight and it made no sense to keep them on the payroll. So, he was a bad expense.

Now, if I could bring in a new employee that could produce as much as the other nine individually, then we would be back to a good expense and a system that made sense again. And if this employee could produce as much as the other nine employees, it could drive my profit margin up to almost 52%.

The thing is we need to do these kinds of figures with every expense in our lives, personal or business. Now personal will be a little different simply because a lot of the things you spend your personal money on will not actually make you any money in return. However, that doesn't mean you have to be stupid about it.

For instance, you have to eat, but you don't have to eat out every single night of the week or every day during lunch. If you figure the average family of four spends $146 to $289 a week (according to *USA Today*) to eat, that is really not that much money. Even if you go on the high side and use the $289 number that breaks down to $41 a day and $14 a meal. That is about $10 per person each day and a little over $3.00 a meal.

Now think about eating out for that. It's not going to happen. If you eat out even one time a day you may take that expense from $289 a week to almost double at $569. That is just figuring $10 a person for some dinner seven days a week. We just need to be vigilant of how we use our money and not create unnecessary expenses for no reason.

Another one I love to hear is when someone says they don't have any money to pay this or pay that, yet they are smoking a cigarette as they are telling me. If you only knew how many times I have gone to collect rent and the person comes to the door to explain to me they have no money to pay the rent this month. Yet, there they stand smoking a cigarette. Then I look inside and see their TV is three times larger than the one I have, and the heat is at 80 degrees. I mean give me a break!

An average cost for a pack of cigarettes in Ohio is $6.03 per pack. And that doesn't include sales tax. So even at one pack a day that is about $2,200 a year. How can you convince me that you can spend $2,200 a year for something that is killing you, but you cannot afford to give you and your kid's shelter? It just blows me away each time I hear it. And don't get me wrong, I don't care if you smoke. That is your choice, but I do care if you tell me you don't have money and you smoke. If you want to smoke and you cannot afford it, then stop telling people how broke you are!

Having expenses in our personal lives is just a part of living this life. But we do have a choice on how large or small the majority of those expenses are. We get to choose where we live and what our housing will cost us. We get to choose what we drive, what we buy, where we go on vacation, what we do for leisure activities, what we eat and so on.

Now some expenses are kind of set. For example, we don't get to choose what price we pay for electric, water, sewer, or fuel for our car. However, we get to decide how much we use each service. If my thermostat is at 75 degrees in the winter and I complain about a high gas or electric bill, I may want to consider a blanket. If I am filling up my car three times a week just to drive around, I may want to reconsider where I am going.

Even with some of our set expenses we still have a choice to make. Using your money wisely demands you do this. If you want to be financially free you must understand what you have coming in and going out. It's really that simple. We are the ones who get to make a lot of these decisions and it's up to us whether or not we have money at the end of each month.

Budgeting

Starting a budget is almost a complete necessity in being financially free. I'm sure someone can pull it off without a budget, but it's a hell of a lot easier if you can see it on paper. A budget is simple. It is putting your income and your expenses on a sheet of paper. It doesn't even need to be anything fancy. It just needs to be something that will show you where your money is going. Below is an example of a very simple budget.

SIMPLE BUDGET

Monthly Income:	*$2500*
Expenses:	
Vehicle	*-$400*
Mortgage	*-$800*
Entertainment	*-$150*
Cell Phone	*-$100*
Utilities	*-$300*

Savings	*-$200*
Food	*-$500*
Total Expenses	**-$2,450**
Total money at end of month	**$50**

Now, again this is a very simple example, but it gives you an idea of how a budget works. A budget can get very complicated and definitely will the more you get into investing, savings, giving, etc.

The good thing is that in this day and age there are so many tools available that can help you to track your money and set up a budget. Microsoft Excel, Everydollar.com, or Mint.com are all great options to help you in starting a budget. You can even use some of them to pull information directly from your bank accounts or investment accounts.

Once you begin to see where your money is going, you will get addicted to watching it. And I think that's a good thing. You will want to know where every penny went and why it went there. You will notice if something is off immediately. You go from dreading doing it to actually looking forward to it. And once you begin investing and seeing your money work for you, it gets even worse (in a good way, of course).

Budgeting just makes sense. If most of us just sat down and went through our money, and our checking account it would blow our minds on how much money we spend on certain things. We would be shocked to see that we waste so much and don't even realize it. Knowing where your money is going is one of the first steps you must take in your financial success.

Paying Taxes

I don't like paying taxes, but who does? I've never heard anyone wake up on April 15th all giddy singing, "I can't wait to pay my taxes today." That's not going to happen. But the truth is there are a couple guarantees in this life. One is you're going to die, the other is you are going to pay taxes. So, you might as well get used to it.

Think about it like this. In order to pay taxes, you had to make money somewhere. I had an older friend of mine tell me once he didn't mind paying taxes. He said, "I would be happy to pay $300,000 in taxes a year." I used to look at him like he was crazy. He would say, "You know why?" I would say "Nope!"

He then proceeded to tell me that if he had to pay $300,000 in taxes then that meant he made about a million dollars that year. He said, "that's still $700,000 in my pocket."

I heard him say this to another buddy of mine once and my other buddy said, "Yeah, but I still don't want to pay that much." I remember him saying, "Well, any day you want to give me a million dollars and I give you $300,000 back, I'll take it."

He was making a point that yes, taxes have to be paid and you will pay them. But don't say dumb things like you don't care if you made a million or not; you still don't want to pay the taxes on it. I agree with him. I'd be happy to pay $300,000 in taxes every year.

On the other end of the spectrum are the people who always seem to get an $8,000 refund at the end of the year. You are always wondering how in the hell that happened? I mean, you paid in and no one gave you anything at the end of the year.

I've had that argument with people as well. They would say how nice it must be for these people to get that kind of money back while they paid in that much. The thing they are not thinking about is the people getting that kind of money back is a family of four making $25,000 a year. I would much rather make $75,000 a year and have to pay in $8,000 than making $25,000 and get $8,000. I don't care if they get $8,000 at the end of the year or not. I plan on continuing making money and paying in. I don't want a refund. That means I didn't make crap that year or I need to reevaluate how much taxes are being taken out of my paycheck.

I had a guy tell me once that "perspective is reality." He was basically saying everyone has their own views, opinions, and ideas and it truly does become reality to them. Sometimes people's reality makes my head hurt, but nonetheless, it's the way they think. I, on the other hand, will continue the path I have chosen of working hard, spending smart, investing wisely and paying my taxes.

CHAPTER 8
WHAT ARE INVESTMENTS?

It's funny when you listen to some people talk about money or how they have "invested" it. I had a tenant a few years ago tell me a mind-blowing story. She was telling me about how she and her husband had been down to their last $50 and weren't sure what they were going to do. (Luckily, this was after she had paid her rent that month). She said all of a sudden, she and her husband had a great idea! They decided it would be wise to go to the nearest convenient store and "invest" their $50 in lottery tickets.

I mean, what could go wrong? They had $50 worth of chances to win. Well, she said they ended up going in and decided they needed some chips and pop (that seems like another completely logical thing to buy with your last $50.) So, they only had about $40 left to put into lottery tickets. They went to the store, got their chips and pop and their $40 worth of lottery tickets. They went back to the car and began scratching, just hoping they would hit it big, hoping their luck would change. And besides, this was an investment.

I mean, they could have just put it all on pop and chips. (This was her logic.) So halfway through, they scratch a winning ticket! They were super excited! Unfortunately, it was only the one ticket that won, but that was okay. They had just won $20! So they rushed back in and *bam*, they get their $20 bill and leave the store.

Now, as she's telling me this, my face is probably twitching uncontrollably in disbelief. My head is hurting and I'm trying to keep my true feelings inside. When she is finished I said, "So, it ended up not being such a great choice then?" She looked me dead in the eye and said, "No, it was a great choice. We made $20 off of it."

My mind was completely blown! I mean how fricken stupid can someone be? You spent $40 to make $20 and, in your head, that is a smart choice? Even in my worst financial mindset, I couldn't get on board with that sort of ignorance. How can someone losing half of their money think they made a good "investment" as she called it?

This takes a true moron! Now granted, this sort of dumbass investment doesn't take a genius to see is stupid. Unfortunately, there are actually people that are this ignorant in the world making financial decisions like this for their families on a daily basis.

I had another guy I knew that told me going to the casino and playing cards was a great investment. And again, he was dead ass serious. He told me that he understood how to do it and he was almost guaranteed to win. He would take a large portion of his weekly check and "invest" it into his card playing abilities.

This all started because he had hit a couple of good hands on some previous days; so now he had convinced himself he was an expert in the card playing field. I remember saying how there were thousands of people every day that played cards and that there were actually even professional card players that have spent thousands, if not millions, to get to where they are.

I explained to him that they have people that back them because these guys do this every day and that is all they do. I asked him how do *you* compete against someone like that? He really had no answer and shockingly enough he didn't make it big in the poker world. As a matter of fact, he basically lost his weekly paycheck a number of times and decided that maybe this wasn't the great investment he thought it was after all.

The crazy thing is people think a lot of times, just because they risk money into something, that it is an investment. Just because you take a chance with money doesn't make it an investment. Gambling can be defined as "taking risky action in the hope of a desired result." Basically, you are taking a chance that something will happen. You are hoping, not investing.

Investing can be described as "expending money with the expectation of achieving a profit or material result by putting it into financial schemes, shares, or property, or by using it to develop a commercial venture."

Investing is not gambling. Investing is putting your money into something that has a proven track record of some sort of a financial return. It's not just throwing money at a lottery or at a casino game and hoping for a good outcome, it's so much more.

Investing takes a lot of research, time and dedication. I mean, Warren Buffett didn't just become one of the richest men in the world in one day. It took him sixty years to create his wealth. It took time, perseverance, education, research, patience and extreme dedication. Just because someone tells you an investment is good, it's not. You have to know what you are buying, (investing in), what it is, what its purpose is, how it works, what return you should make, what others have made off of it and basically everything you can learn about it. It has to make sense. I've seen too many people get into something they know absolutely nothing about just because someone else said it was a good idea.

Stocks Investing

I remember to this day the first time I had ever really even heard of the stock market, or at least when I cared enough to acknowledge its existence. A buddy of mine was sitting at his computer at our real estate office and he was trading stocks online.

This really intrigued me. I had no idea how it worked, how to do it or honestly, what it really was. So, he showed me a little bit of what was going on. At that time, he had invested in Kroger stock and he showed me how he had bought the stock at like $27 and it was now up to $29 just a couple months later. He had made

$2 a share or 7% in just two short months. That is a pretty decent return on average.

So, I began to ask him a lot more questions, pick his brain and do the research myself. I really wanted to understand how this investing in the stock market worked. I mean, how many times have you heard of these Wall Street guys making millions or even billions off of the stock market. So, I kept researching how it worked and finally opened my own online account.

I remember telling my buddy that I was about to do it and was asking him how much money to put in? At that time in my life, I didn't have a lot at all. He suggested I put in $1000. That was a lot of money to me at that point in my life and it scared me to death. But I scraped up the money (sold some things and didn't use credit) and put my first $1,000 in. I remember my buddy saying if you lose it just think of it as $1000 tuition to the school of learning the stock market.

The thing is we have to educate ourselves on everything we invest our money into. I always like to describe investing as "my money making me more money." I want each dollar I put into an investment to have a purpose. And fifteen years ago, I had no idea what a good investment even looked like.

Now, after trial and error, much reading and self-educating through experiences, gains, losses, etc. I have done thousands of investments.

Stock investing is not quite as simple as it sounds. I have been watching stocks for years and just when you think you picked a great one, something will happen within the company or something out of the company's control (some sort of economic decline) and the stock will plummet. This is why it is never wise to put more into single stocks than you can afford to lose.

When you are buying stock in a company, you are actually buying a piece or a percentage of that company. So that means you actually own a percentage of whatever company that is. Some companies pay a dividend (typically a quarterly profit sharing) which can increase your growth and/ or income from the company. But again, not all stocks pay dividends.

Whenever investing in single stocks, you must make sure you understand what you actually are buying or what you own. I have seen too many people I've known buy into a company and have no idea what the company even does. You have to know what services or products the company produces or provides, as well as how the company is doing financially and if it pays a dividend.

Now, just because the company doesn't pay a dividend, doesn't mean you shouldn't invest in it; the dividend can just be a perk. It just depends on what your financial goals are. I heard a guy once say you should never invest in anything that you don't understand. I couldn't agree more. If you don't get it, then don't get in it!

Bad Investments

Besides the obvious gambling investments, there are other scams you can get caught up into as well. I have known some really good people who have lost thousands of dollars in things like penny stocks, scams, Ponzi schemes etc. Actually, as we speak, I am predicting (in my opinion) that the cryptocurrency bubble is about to burst.

Usually, if an investment sounds too good to be true, it is. To make thousand percent returns is completely unsustainable. The math just simply does not work. People can sell speculation, but that doesn't make something a good investment either. Something like this is gambling.

Penny stocks are a prime example of this and so is the cryptocurrency market we are currently seeing. People are taking out mortgages, credit card debt, and equity lines and then buying on margin. This is a guaranteed way to lose all you have, more than you have and put yourself into bankruptcy.

This is not investing; this is trying to get rich quick. The people who buy in this late will lose the most, unfortunately. Now, that doesn't mean that some people can't make money off these sorts of things and as a matter of fact, the first ones in can even become very wealthy. But typically, a lot of people investing in these types of things ultimately lose a lot more than they even ever had.

Money with a Purpose

We have to keep our money safe. Think how hard it is for us to get our money in the first place. How many hours we work, how many days and all the time we put in. To throw it in the trash (which is basically what we are doing if we gamble in things we don't understand) is completely stupid and irresponsible. We have to take better care of what we have.

Penny stocks are not the only bad investments out there. Unfortunately, there are many bad investments in every market and sometimes an entire market can be considered a bad investment for a period of time. In the crash of 2008, people would not buy anything. They were staying away from real estate, stocks, bonds, mutual funds, you name it. Basically, people were going to cash. Now I believe in buying when others are selling, but again, you have to be wise about it. Some of the biggest profits I've made were when others are freaking out.

However, it is not always that simple either. You still need to understand what you are buying and what is causing it to go down at the current time; the time of purchase.

Like I was telling you earlier in this book, I had a professor that had bought into the real estate bubble. Once he passed away, his wife had to end up filing for bankruptcy. This is why we have to be wise in what we buy. We also need to pay off debt (even business debt) as quickly as possible.

We need to reinvest in our properties, stocks, businesses etc... If we get rid of debt and reinvest in our investments it just speeds up the process of becoming financially free. If you invest and take your profits out of the investment and blow them, then you are losing out on so much potential growth. You can be compounding your money, but instead, you are blowing the returns and it decreases your growth potential by a significant amount.

Mutual Funds

There is an endless amount of great investments out there in this world. And like I said, they come in all different shapes and sizes. If you have investments in many different areas, then you are well diversified. Diversifying your investments simply means that you have a variety of investments.

In other words, you don't have all your eggs in one basket. It is extremely important when you invest to have your portfolio very diversified. You want to have as many different assets and asset classes in your portfolio as you can. This will help you in a market downturn or correction and can help you with the potential loss of a single investment.

A few years back, I bought this one stock. It was a single stock. The company was (SeaDrill) SDRL. Now at the time, oil was doing great at over a $100 a barrel and SDRL was trading at $40 and paying over a 10% dividend. Well, one-day, oil was forecasted to drop the following year and SDRL was leveraged with a very high debt load. They had borrowed a lot based on oil staying at current levels and were overextended if oil prices began to fall.

Well, that's exactly what happened. They ended up cutting their dividend to zero which made investors dump their stock within days. Just a couple years later, that same stock that was trading at $40+ dollars a share now trades at $0.24 cents a share. That's right, $0.24 cents a share within just a few years. In other words, the company lost over 99% of its value in a very short time period.

This lesson cost me a lot of money and as a matter of fact, I hated it in a very bad way. But even someone like me who has been investing for a long time can still make a bad investment. None of us are immune from mistakes. That is why it is wise to be completely diversified in your portfolio. The good thing for me is that this was a very small percentage of my overall portfolio, so it didn't affect me that much at all. However, if this was my only money and the only investment, it could have sunk me. This is why you have to be wise when investing and do your research.

Mutual funds and index funds are some of my favorite things to invest in, especially if you are new to investing. Single stocks can be so volatile and risky, but a mutual fund or index fund takes a lot of this risk out. Now don't get me wrong, there is a risk in every investment that you put your money into, but these sorts of funds just reduce the risk for you.

A mutual fund is an investment program funded by shareholders that trade in diversified holdings and is professionally managed. In other words, it is something with a large number of companies (stocks) within one investment. So, if one of the stocks within the fund's value goes down, the idea is the other stock's values within the fund will not go down.

You can find mutual funds with all kinds of companies in them. A mutual fund will have companies from financials and energy, to retail and real estate, and to services and so on. Some funds are sector specific and for the most part, I would suggest staying away from these types of funds. I suggest getting a few different funds (especially starting out) that will have international stocks, US Large Cap stocks, Midcap and Small cap stocks. Basically, the Large, Mid and Small Caps are just the different sizes of the companies ranging from very large companies like Amazon to very small companies that may have potential growth over the years. But again, you want to make sure you do your homework.

With mutual funds, you can look back through the history and find funds that have had 9% or 10% growth on average over a ten year period or even more. Now that doesn't mean that they will always do that, remember it's an average. One year the return may be 17% and the next year it may be 7%.

The idea is that over a twenty to thirty-year time frame, these funds will average out a return of 10% or so, that will compound and make your money grow.

As I spoke about earlier, reinvesting is key to financial success. You must reinvest your dividends and I suggest investing money into your funds on a weekly basis. There are a number of ways you can do this from 401K's to Roth IRA's to OPERS, STRS and so on. If you have an employer-funded account, I would suggest maxing it out and taking advantage of the employer's contribution to a maximum capacity. This will help accelerate your retirement funds and investments by far and get you to financial freedom a lot quicker.

CHAPTER 9
COMPOUND INTEREST

Now with all that being said about investments, the secret formula (which is not a secret at all) is compound interest. That is how all of this works. Compound interest is the result of reinvesting interest, rather than paying it out, so that interest in the next period is then earned on the principal sum plus previously-accumulated interest.

Albert Einstein viewed compound interest like this:

"Compound interest is the eighth wonder of the world. He who understands it earns it . . . he who doesn't . . . pays it."

"Compound interest is the most powerful force in the universe."

"Compound interest is the greatest mathematical discovery of all time."

In other words, you continue putting money in, but the interest you earn (if left in the investment) will be added to the principal and will continue to grow more and more each day, week, month and year.

Warren Buffett, the most famous and successful investor of all time, used compound Interest and reinvesting to watch his wealth skyrocket from the age of fifty-two to eighty-seven. Warren Buffett had a net worth of 376 million at age fifty-two and by using the principles of compound interest and time is now, (at the age of eighty-seven years old) worth approximately 84 billion dollars. The beautiful thing about compound interest is the more money that is accumulated; the quicker it gets to massive numbers.

Now granted, Warren Buffett has made a significant amount of money that most of us will only ever dream of, but the principles are the same. Most of us can definitely be wealthy by simply saving and investing over a twenty to thirty-year period of time. And I am talking about normal, everyday people like me and you.

Take for example a teacher that makes a salary of $50,000 a year. Let's say that the teacher puts in 10% of their income every year which is $5,000 a year or about $416 a month. Now let's say that their employer gives them a 3% a year match (an additional $1500 a year or $125 a month) so now the teacher is putting in a total of $416+125=$541 a month into their retirement. So, they invest the $541 a month into a few different mutual funds within their retirement vehicle that will hopefully give them an average of 10% return a year.

Over a thirty-year period, that teacher now has $1,124,897.00. So just by simply investing 10% of their income, they have become a millionaire in a thirty-year period. So, if this teacher started teaching right out of college at the age of twenty-two, they can be worth over a million dollars by the time they are fifty-two years old. If that same teacher would have just put that money into a savings account with basically no interest, that same $416 a month (with no employer match) for a thirty-year period, they would only have about $150,000. See a significant difference? That's almost a million dollars lost just because they didn't use compound interest.

I know it sounds too good to be true, but fortunately, it isn't! Anyone who is willing to take the time and just put in a small portion of their income on a weekly basis can do this with time. I wish someone would have told me this when I was fifteen years old or even twenty or twenty-five. I didn't begin any investing until later. But if we teach our kids this tool, they can become millionaires quicker than any of us could ever have imagined.

Just look back at Warren Buffett. He started with a net worth of $5000 when he was fourteen. Now, that is still a lot of money, especially at fourteen, but he worked for his money when he was that young with paper routes and a pinball machine business that he started.

My point is if we work and teach our kids to work and we invest and teach our kids to invest, we can almost all achieve financial freedom. We are the main cause of us not becoming financially free.

Compound Interest in Reverse

In today's society and the world, instead of using compound interest to work for us as Warren Buffett has and thousands of other very successful investors have, we actually do the opposite and reverse compound interest to work against us. Just as Alert Einstein said in his quote:

"Compound interest is the eighth wonder of the world. He who understands it earns it . . . he who doesn't . . . pays it."

For example, we take out mortgages, credit cards, student loans, vehicle loans, and lines of credit and so on. Well, guess what? This is compound interest in reverse. Instead of you paying yourself and using the compounding of interest in your favor, you are actually compounding the bank's money for them by paying them interest on principal and in turn, they can actually reinvest and have your money (their money now) compound even further.

You have heard it said that the rich get richer and the poor get poorer. Well, that is a very true statement, but in most cases, it's caused by our own poor decisions. Now I am not saying this is every case because there are some issues families' face that will not allow them to save and invest, but in most cases, we live way beyond our means.

Instead of driving the car that is a few years old that we could save and pay for, we chose to pay payments of $500 or even more a month on a brand new one. At Christmas time we chose to spend on credit cards to buy gifts that will be forgotten within days or weeks after being purchased. We spend tomorrow's money and when you spend tomorrow's money it not only takes away from your availability to save and invest today, it also causes reverse compound interest in your life.

When you're paying compound interest, you are paying interest on top of principal and interest. So, if you are borrowing money on, a credit card of $1000 and are paying an interest rate of 17% compounded annually, you ultimately end up paying the credit card back $1486 if you pay the minimum $25 payment for a five-year period. The only way to become financially free is to stop spending tomorrow's money and buy only what we can afford today.

I know a lot of times we have heard that we need to live within our means. Well, I am going to take it a step further and say we should live below our means. To me, living within my means is simply saying don't spend more than you make.

That is good advice, but that doesn't make you a millionaire. Living below your means does. If I live within my means, I have no extra money to put towards savings and investing. I basically see the money come in and watch it go back out every single month. I live a fine life, but I never really get ahead.

Now if I live below my means, it paints an entirely different picture. Sure, I may not have everything on the earth I would like to right now. But, living below my means gives me the freedom to be able to save for a rainy day and also gives me the freedom of investing. It gives me the availability to use compound interest in my favor and allow my money to work for me.

So instead of watching my money come in every month and simply go back out, now I can watch it continue to grow on a monthly and yearly basis. I can watch my net worth go up every year and know that I am making a better future for me and my family and hopefully change my family tree for the better.

I would far rather watch that then simply seeing my money disappear into the abyss of nonexistence. Not living within or below your means, in my opinion, is simply a waste of great investment opportunities.

CHAPTER 10
MAKING YOUR MONEY WORK FOR YOU

Your Money is a Tool, So Use it Like One

I think one of the biggest problems with today's society is that no one looks at money as a tool. Sure, we all know we go to work, we put in our forty hours and then on Friday we pick up our paychecks to cash them just to do it all again the following week. But we look at money as something to spend on things we want. I mean, I guess for some that could be considered a tool, but I am talking about a tool that actually works for you to create more wealth.

A few weeks ago, I was talking to one of my buddies and he was talking about spending money on this or that and buying something new. As I listened, I began to realize that most people simply don't get it. I told him until you can understand how money works you cannot be successful in a financial aspect. He asked what I meant. So, I elaborated.

Money should be viewed as something (a tool) to create more money. It should be viewed as something that you can invest, not spend, and by doing so you have more of it after the transaction. He didn't think this ideology was plausible and, in some instances, he would be correct. But the truth is, in a large number of cases, it can be.

Think of it this way. If for every purchase we made we stepped back and looked at it a little deeper, we could decide how this purchase was going to help us in some way.

Now we know there are the necessities of life that we have no choice but to spend our money on. For example, food, water, shelter, clothing, utilities, transportation and so on. Those things are a given. Without one of these, we cannot continue our lives in a fashion that will most likely allow us to make more money or even possibly survive in some cases.

However, do we need the most expensive car for transportation? I've had some people tell me they have got to have something dependable. And quite frankly I agree with that statement. But the problem is there is a large gap between dependable (something you can afford) and brand new (something most people cannot afford). Or when I hear of someone buying a $100 pair of sunglasses or a $250 purse, or a $100 pair of jeans it drives me insane.

Now, I am not saying some people can't afford this, because some people definitely can. But for the majority of people in this world, they cannot. And unfortunately, there have to be enough "normal" people buying this kind of stuff otherwise the companies making them couldn't stay in business.

I am not advocating that these companies shouldn't be in business. I am just saying most people cannot afford to pay this kind of money for these types of things, but they chose to do so instead of paying themselves first and investing. They put instant gratification at a ten and investing (making your money work for you) at a one or maybe even a zero.

Until we look at a purchase with the vision of what it will make us in return, instead of what it will cost us, I don't believe we can be financially successful. Money is one of the greatest tools and assets we will ever possess. Now that doesn't mean I'm money hungry and saying don't spend on anything. But, I am saying spend most of your money on things that can produce you more money.

It's really not that hard. But the first step in any of this is to be content with what we have and not caring what others have. Until we make peace with those two things we will never even try to use money as a tool.

The Sooner You Invest

In the last couple chapters, we have been talking about investing and compounding interest, what it is, what it means and some of the ways to do it. The thing we have to keep in mind is time. Time is a key component in investing. I know I have shown you a few examples, but we have to always keep in mind that time is so important. I would never say you are too old to begin investing, because I don't believe that. But the sooner you get started, the better off you will be.

This is why I wish they taught this sort of thing in school. Just think, if our kids came home from school and started telling us about stocks, bonds, mutual funds and investing. What if they were so fired up and excited about the lesson they just learned that they wanted to start putting $50 a week away into an investment savings account or a mutual fund. This would begin to change our nation's mindset.

Instead of everyone focusing on all the "stuff" they could buy with their money, maybe they would begin focusing on how to make their money grow. Just imagine showing a teenager that just $50 a week could grow to over $400,000 by the time they were forty-five years old. And that's without ever adding anything else to it. But the beautiful thing would be the ripple effect it would have on them and their children.

If we could teach our kids at a very young age to begin saving and investing, they would most certainly begin adding more money to it when they started making more. Then $50 a week becomes a $100 and then maybe even $200 and all of a sudden, these kids are millionaires' way quicker than we could ever be or quicker than they ever thought possible. And it's simply because they were given something we were not; true investing knowledge.

Money Can Help You or Hurt You

The truth of the matter is it's up to us what we ultimately decide to do with our money. We can take the mindset of our money is a tool to be used to create more money (wealth) or we can choose to see it as a limited resource to buy the things we want. The choice is ours.

A lot of people I know or have met over the years will choose to do just that. They would rather spend every cent they make at their job and criticize the wealthy for being just that. They are in the mindset that somehow these wealthy people with money did not work hard to get where they are. They have the mindset that these people made no sacrifices to be in the financial positions they are today.

The truth of the matter is most wealthy or financially free people have made good decisions, have practiced great patience and have sacrificed more than you could ever imagine or ever would. It's that simple. The ideology that wealthy people were all born with a silver spoon or just woke up one day into wealth is just a fairy tale. Sure, in some instances it has happened, there are exceptions to every rule. But the reality is that in most cases people become wealthy due to hard work, patience, sacrifice, persistence and time.

Money Is Evil

First off, money is not evil. The Bible says it this way.

"For the **LOVE** of money is the root of all evil" (1 Timothy 6:10.)

We first need to get the idea that money is evil out of our heads and realize money can't be evil. Money is an object and money has no feelings; people have feelings. We are the ones that create evil feelings by loving money.

I remember this one time I was in a Bible study at this small church I went to. We were on the subject of money and how to manage your finances in a "Biblical manner." We were discussing how to spend wisely, save wisely, how to try and avoid debt, and not worship money. I remember one girl stating that avoiding debt was almost impossible in this day and age. She went on further to say that the wealthy or the financially free people had it too easy. She said they didn't have to worry about anything and that all they did was worshiped money.

I remember playing the devil's advocate and giving the class a different perspective on the subject matter. I said most wealthy people had worked hard for their money and that they accumulated their wealth because of that. I went on to say that most of the wealthy people didn't believe in debt and that they practiced patience and didn't buy everything they wanted or saw.

I then told the class that I thought some of the poorest people I knew worshiped money way more than most of the wealthy people I knew. The one girl said it's impossible to worship money if you don't have it. I said I truly disagreed with that.

I could see their heads beginning to hurt so I explained. I said think about it. A lot of everyday people (the working poor) worship the idea of money. They worship wanting "stuff" and will try and get it at any cost. They will put their financial security at risk, their families at risk, their homes at risk and sometimes even their health at risk, just to have the next newest thing. That could be a vehicle, a TV, a living room suite, a boat, a motorcycle and the list goes on.

They may not have the money to actually buy something, but they can sure buy it on credit. So instead of practicing patience, they give into the trap of credit and instant gratification. They are a true example of someone worshiping money in order to get "stuff!"

Even after my explanation, you could see that most of them (if not all of them) disagreed with my point of view. They didn't get it because if you get it, you have to admit to yourself that you fall into that category. And if you do that, you have no choice, but to say you worship money and "stuff" as well or choose to be content. Neither one of those things is easy to do.

My point is this. People love to point the finger. We love to blame everyone else for our mistakes and for our misfortunes. Now, don't get me wrong. Some people have had really tough lives due to circumstances out of their control.

But the majority of us can control what happens to us. We can control what we do with our money and how we spend it. We can decide if we need to finance that new car or buy one we can afford. I mean vehicles used to be a means of transportation and now we have made it something to show people how great we are doing.

We have choices in our lives, and unfortunately, most of us will make the wrong ones with our finances (even after reading a hundred common sense books like this one.) We just don't want to change. We just don't want to be content. It's just too hard. It's so much easier to buy what we want now on credit than be content. We would rather buy now and complain how hard we have it then save for later and be financially free.

The funny thing is, once you begin to practice contentment in your life, you will quickly realize that most of the spur of the moment "stuff" you want, after just a few days you could care less about. That is why stores try and get you to buy at the point of purchase. They want you to buy it the second you see it and not go home and think about it. They know if you don't purchase it right then, the actual chances of you coming back to purchase it is almost zero.

We have a really simple choice to make. Be content, start saving and practice patience or keep spending like a drunken sailor. Money is a tool no matter what. The choice is ours. Will we use this tool to work for us and help us build wealth or will we spend it all and use it to buy more "stuff" and allow it to be a tool for someone else to use.

CHAPTER 11
WHY GIVING IS CRITICAL/CRUCIAL TO BEING FINANCIALLY SUCCESSFUL

One of the most satisfying things in life you can do is giving back. I know some of you are thinking that I have lost my mind and are trying to figure out how in the world giving away your money can even remotely help you in any fashion to being financially free. Well, bear with me and I will explain.

We've all heard of Warren Buffett and Bill Gates, correct? I mean unless you've been living under a rock you should know these names when someone says them. These are two of the wealthiest men in the entire world.

Warren Buffett, as we know, is considered to be the greatest investor of all time; making billions off of investing in companies and practicing patience over a very long period of time.

Bill Gates is the founder of Microsoft. He created something out of nothing and has created massive amounts of wealth and has even been declared the richest man in the world.

Now some of you might think, oh, lucky them! It must be nice to have all that money. These rich guys are greedy and have gotten all of their money because of greed.

Well, guess what? You couldn't be more mistaken. Both of these guys and many others just like them started from nothing. They worked their way out of nothing to become known as some of the wealthiest people of all time.

But you want to hear the most interesting part? Both of these very wealthy people have given billions, that's right billions, of dollars away to charities and to help all sorts of people who are less fortunate than they are. Now I know you're probably thinking, of course, they can give away billions of dollars because they have billions more.

Warren Buffett has given away an estimated $24 billion and his current net worth is $84 billion and Bill Gates, whose net worth is currently $90 billion has given away an estimated $28 billion. Now, let me ask you this. If you currently had $90,000 would you be willing to just give $28,000 of it away and get nothing in return?

The answer is most likely no.

But these guys have been giving away billions of dollars for years. And the best part is they have created a foundation where they have gotten 154 other billionaires (10% of all billionaires) to pledge to give away at least half of their wealth when they die. Warren Buffett and Bill Gates have both pledged to give away 99% of their wealth when they die.

Just think of that. The money these people have worked for their entire lives they are willing to donate in the billions to people and foundations for no self-gain at all. They won't be giving it to family members to squander away, but rather to people or foundations that are in desperate need of it.

They are doing it because that is how a lot of wealthy people think. They think a lot different than the average person. As "working poor" Americans, we are taught that the wealthy are the enemy. We are taught they are evil and are trying to keep us down. Well for the most part, that couldn't be any further from the truth. Most of these people that have created wealth would love to share how they did it or what some of their tricks are. They would love to help you succeed, but the truth is most of us would never take their advice and just go back to complaining as we always have.

Wealthy people give, not only because it's the right thing to do, but also because they want to. Most wealthy people are so grateful for what they have, and they want to share it with others. They know there are people less fortunate than them and they are happy to help out. I know some of the greatest feelings I've ever experienced is helping out families who are less fortunate than I am.

I remember this one time there was a girl at my church who had posted something on Facebook about a family with a single mom that had two kids that needed some school clothes. The girl who made the post said they were just asking for a few used items to get by.

I saw this as a teaching opportunity, so I got my three little girls and we went shopping. I had the girls pick out five outfits for each child. The girls loved doing it, just knowing some little kids would be so happy to have new clothes. I remember when we took them to the girl at church and told her to give them to the family. She couldn't believe we went out and bought new clothes. I told her we were blessed and simply glad to do it.

A few weeks later, this girl at church brought me a card from the mom of this family we had helped. In the card the message was simple. It said something along the lines of "we appreciate what you did so much! The kids never dreamed they would have new clothes for school."

The part that got me though was the ending. She said, "Why would you do this for us? You don't even know us."

When I read that part, it brought me to tears. I would have loved to answer her, but to this day I have never met the girl with two kids. And I didn't do it for self-gratification. I did it because there was a need and it was the right thing to do. I did it because sometimes all of us need a little help. I have been blessed and I wanted to pass it on to someone else.

It just feels really good to be able to help people when you can. And the best part is the more financially free you become, the more people you can help.

Giving Shows Stability

From a financial perspective, giving simply shows stability. If you can afford to give it means you have more than you need (in most cases.) Now I am not saying some people don't give more than they can afford. I mean there are actually people who have done this multiple times throughout history.

But for the sake of this argument, in most cases if someone is giving, they can afford to do so. And if you can afford to give, then you must have at least made some halfway decent decisions with your money. I mean if you are willing to help out another family, or a foundation, or just someone in need, it is presumed that you have the extra money to do so.

Giving shows stability in the sense that you manage your money well. It shows that you are content with what you have and are not taking every single penny you make and trying to use it on yourself for the newest and nicest "stuff."

Think about it. If you were still in the mindset of always wanting to spend and buy everything you could for yourself, then giving to someone else wouldn't even cross your mind. So, you have now begun to at least show some contentment in your life. You are also putting other's needs above yourself. You are taking a back seat to your wants and desires and are putting someone else's needs before them.

Stability is key to giving. It's so neat to see a person who changes from a greedy person (as we are taught to be in America) to a giving, kind-hearted person. It's just such a neat transformation. This person who has never given anything before is now getting addicted to it. And the best part is, once you begin giving, you can't help but want to do it more and more. It just feels so right and so nice to be able to help people who are less fortunate then you are.

Giving Is Not Good In All Instances

Now, I know throughout this book I have talked about people being greedy, people spending their money on dumb things and people just being completely irresponsible with their money. And the unfortunate thing is, these people will not only ask you to give to them, once you begin to become financially successful, they will expect it.

I remember when I first started to make a little bit more money than I ever had before, some of the people I knew would just pretty much beg me for my money. Now at first, I seemed to always just help out (give it away) without asking.

But I quickly realized that in doing this, it just created this monster that made them keep coming back. Now they saw me as an ATM machine. It went from helping people to supporting them. And everyone had a sob story to explain why they needed this or that. You have to be wise in giving. People will take advantage of you. And yes, even family, friends and people you trust.

There are most definitely people who cannot help themselves, but that's not always the case. People will take advantage of you if you allow them too. I remember this one time I helped this family buy propane for their house. They had a few kids and said they had no heat. So, I gave them money to have their propane tank filled and help them out. Just a few days later, I saw this same person on social media posting photos of the new jewelry and clothes they had just bought.

Now it seems kind of funny to me that just a few days ago they were out of heating fuel, but now they have new clothes and jewelry. People don't care about your money like you do.

The story I just told you reminds me of a show I used to watch called *I Love Raymond.* I'm sure a lot of you have seen it. In the one episode, Ray gave Robert, I believe, $1,000 to help him pay his bills. Robert was saying how he was broke and stressed out because of it. So, Ray gave him money.

Well, Ray found out a few days later that Robert was going on a weekend trip to Vegas. Ray was livid. He confronted Robert and Robert said yes, he was going to Vegas. Ray said, "I thought you didn't have any extra money?" Robert replied, "I didn't until you gave me $1,000." Robert said, "I'm not using your $1000 for Vegas. I used your $1,000 for the bills and I'm using my $1,000 for Vegas."

That's about the same scenario as this person I helped. In Ray and Robert's case, Robert took advantage of someone willing to help him out and so did the person I helped.

The one story is a fictional TV series, but the other is not. People will most certainly take advantage of you if you allow them to. And believe me, I have learned that the hard way multiple times. And most of the time it's by people you thought would never do it and are even sometimes friends and family.

Just because someone tells you they need money doesn't mean you have to give it. I suggest you give money to respectable charities. Now that doesn't mean I am saying don't give any money to individuals. I am just saying be wise and make sure you understand the situation as best as you can. And if someone comes back to you multiple times, then it is time to cut them off.

Sometimes helping individuals is the best thing you can do. Just like the one family who I bought school clothes for appreciated it more than I may ever know. But sometimes it blows up like the other family I donated money to in order to fill their propane tank. In the one instance, the family needed school clothes and I never even met them and they never asked me for anything again. They appreciated it wholeheartedly and sent me a card stating that.

In the other example the family needed heat. They used my money to buy heat and their money to buy "stuff." They did not appreciate it but rather expected it and actually tried multiple times after that to get me to "help" them again.

I refused. I mean, it is a shame that we have to even think that people would try and take advantage of someone that is giving or willing to help them, but unfortunately, it happens all the time.

Another one of the biggest issues in the area I live in is the drug epidemic. It seems like every week you hear of multiple overdoses, people stealing, breaking into houses, and getting busted for shooting up. It's unfortunate and it seems like every family around my small town has been touched in some way by it.

I have a family member who has been addicted to heroin for years. And unfortunately, I have helped out a few times in the beginning stages of their addiction, but I quickly realized that there was no change. I saw multiple other people help to the point of enabling and would even get angry at others that wouldn't help.

But these types of people can only help themselves. Giving them money does nothing but finances their habits and addictions. They don't appreciate it; they just want it to get high. They will steal, cheat, lie and tell you every story in the book to try and take advantage of your generosity. This is why you have to be wise in giving.

Fortunately for my family, this person has been to rehab and jail multiple times, but at present time appears to be on the road to recovery. I hope and pray that is the case. Not only for them, their health and their kids, but for the many people who have been taken advantage of by their generous nature.

Giving Is Biblical

I know some of you are reading my *Giving is Biblical* right now and thinking "Here we go!" This book is not designed to be a Biblical book, but I certainly believe that the Bible does teach us to be smart and responsible with our finances. And I believe in doing so, it teaches us that giving is not only a good thing to do, but it is expected. I also believe that we are blessed when we give back to others. The Bible says:

"He who supplies seed to the sower and bread for food will supply and multiply your seed for sowing and increase the harvest of your righteousness. You will be enriched in every way for all your generosity, which through us will produce thanksgiving to God. For the ministry of this service is not only supplying the needs of the saints but is also overflowing in many thanksgivings to God" **(2 Cor. 9:6-12 ESV.)**

I look at this verse as saying if you give, God is going to bless you for it. And no, I do not believe in a health and wealth kind of giving, I am simply saying that I believe God blesses us for blessing others. I believe a lot of it is motive as well.

I mean if I go out today (or anyone for that matter) and give $10,000 and plan on getting seven times my money back and look at it as a guaranteed investment; I think I've lost not only my mind, but the entire reason the Bible talks about giving. There is a reason we are blessed with giving. We are blessed from giving because we give without expecting anything in return.

In my opinion, if you give to someone with the motivation that you are getting something back then you will never be blessed. You have to give because you want to give. You have to give and expect that you will have nothing come back to you. And in my experience, this is when you will be blessed.

Here are a few other verses I really like about helping and giving to the less fortunate.

(Proverbs 19:17 ESV)

Whoever is generous to the poor lends to the Lord, and he will repay him for his deed.

(Proverbs 22:9 ESV)

Whoever has a bountiful eye will be blessed, for he shares his bread with the poor.

(Acts 20:35 ESV)

In all things, I have shown you that by working hard in this way we must help the weak and remember the words of the Lord Jesus, how he himself said, 'It is more blessed to give than to receive.'

(Luke 14:12-14 ESV)

He said also to the man who had invited him, 'when you give a dinner or a banquet, do not invite your friends or your brothers or your relatives or rich neighbors, lest they also invite you in return and you be repaid. But when you give a feast, invite the poor, the crippled, the lame, the blind, and you will be blessed, because they cannot repay you. For you will be repaid at the resurrection of the just.'

(Deuteronomy 15:11 ESV)

For there will never cease to be poor in the land. Therefore, I command you, 'You shall open wide your hand to your brother, to the needy and to the poor, in your land.'

(Proverbs 14:21 ESV)

Whoever despises his neighbor is a sinner but blessed is he who is generous to the poor.

(Luke 3:11 ESV)

And he answered them, "Whoever has two tunics is to share with him who has none, and whoever has food is to do likewise."

Now, I didn't give you these verses to give you a Bible lesson, but rather to make a point. When we are blessed, God calls us to bless others. And as I stated before, I believe we will be blessed because of it. God knows our hearts and I believe He can see a generous heart that has no self-motives vs. someone who is giving for their own gain.

If you don't believe in the Bible, then that is up to you, but I choose to believe in it. But again, this book is not designed to change your belief system or religious views.

This book is about being wise with your money. Giving does not have to be a Biblical thing if you don't want it to be. Some people believe in Karma or "what goes around comes around".

My point is this. Whatever your belief system, giving should just be a part of who and what we are. This world is full of people who are less fortunate than we are (especially as Americans) and we should be happy to help people out who are in true need.

Now, as I said before, this doesn't mean giving away to "takers" or people who are looking to take advantage of your generosity but giving to people who truly need the help.

To me, there will never be a feeling that even compares to giving something to someone in need. Imagine the feeling you get when you see your little girl open that new baby doll under the Christmas tree or when your little boy sees his brand-new baseball glove.

That is the same sort of feeling you get when you help someone who truly needs it. You are giving for no reason other than you want to help. You have no other motives. They are receiving also with no motives, they are just less fortunate or down on their luck. To me, this is true giving!

CHAPTER 12
WHY ALMOST ANYONE WITH A JOB CAN BECOME A MILLIONAIRE

I will always stick by the statement that almost anyone with a job and someone who has patience and is willing to work can achieve millionaire status. Now, I know the skeptics are reading this right now saying "yeah, right." But I'm here to tell you it is not only possible, but very plausible.

Throughout this book, I have shown you simple common-sense insights about self-discipline, money management and investing. I have given you real-life examples and ideas.

Becoming a millionaire, in my opinion, is a choice. Now again, there are certain instances where people may have personal disabilities or life circumstances where this may not be the case. But in most cases if you have a job, save and spend wisely, and invest in simple mutual funds over time you can most definitely achieve millionaire status.

The problem is most people will never do it. It's not that they can't, they simply won't. They don't want to make the changes in their lives that would allow them to do so. They have gotten too comfortable living how they do with two car payments, house payments, credit card debt and just buying everything they want, even if they cannot afford it.

It's kind of like the obese person who goes to the doctor and is told to lose weight. They start off great. They go out and get a gym membership, go to the grocery store and buy a cart full of fresh produce and vegetables and say, "Here we go." Only to notice a few weeks later they went one time to the gym and now they are back to eating chips and cookies and drinking six cans of soda a day. They said they would change, but when push comes to shove, they just don't want to do it. They don't have the will.

Or like another story a buddy of mine told me once. He knew this alcoholic that would drink a lot of alcohol every single day. And I mean a lot. He said this guy would drink all day and even get up in the middle of the night and drink and then go back to sleep. He never drank water or any other beverage for that matter. This guy was a true alcoholic.

Well, he went to the doctor one day and the doctor told him his liver was about to give up on him. It was about to stop working and that if he didn't change his habits and stop drinking, he would ultimately die from liver failure. He was drinking himself to death.

My buddy told me the guy didn't even make it a day and decided the doctor didn't know what he was talking about. He said doctors don't know everything and he went back to the exact same lifestyle he has been living for years.

My point is that no one wants to change. We get comfortable and we don't want to take advice. We got it in our heads that we know best. We are willing to jeopardize our health and even our lives because we don't want to change.

And to me, that is exactly how we need to look at our financial future. We should look at it as if it is a life or death situation. According to legend, Socrates said to Plato, "Until you want it as much as you want to breathe, you will never have it."

That is true in so many instances in our lives. There is always someone else on the next street over, or the next town over, or even the next state over that wants it more than you.

That's why you have to want it as bad as you want oxygen. You can't just want to win financially, you have to starve for it!

You have to need it like you need oxygen in your lungs. You have to make a conscious decision to work every second you can on it because someone else will put in that extra second, that extra minute or that extra hour. When you want it that bad, that's when you will win.

99% of Being Successful Is Attitude and Mindset

Just as my last statement basically says, wanting to be successful or wanting to win is almost all your attitude. If you want to win badly enough you will. If you are just going at it casually then you will get mediocre results.

The most successful people in this world fail and fail again. The difference is they pick themselves up off the floor, dust themselves off, learn from their mistakes and do it again. Only this time they do it differently. They already know the way they just failed doesn't work so they try something new.

Until you have your mind right, it is impossible to win. You have to eat and breathe this stuff. You have to read about it, talk about it and think about it to the point of annoyance. When you start annoying people because you talk about being financially free so much or being financially successful, that is when you are on the right track.

Most people will never get it so they will not care. They would rather talk about sports games, TV shows, Video games or social media. On the other hand, you want to talk about success, examples of successful people, what the stock market is doing, how much returns you are making on your investments and how much debt you paid off. This is when you are beginning to win!

The problem with most people in this world is that they have been programmed since being a child to do the dead opposite of this. They are taught in school that everyone is a winner and just for participating you achieved something.

Well, I'm here to tell you that is a load of horse SHIT! There are no participation trophies in life. If you want to win, you have to beat someone in order to achieve it. And the thing is you can, you just simply have to be the best at what you do.

My brother worked as a plumber for years and became really good at it. He was a hard worker, and everyone knew it. He decided to open his own company and within the first year he was so covered up with work, he didn't know what to do with it. He was working seven days a week, twelve to sixteen hours a day. It's not because he got lucky, but it's because he worked his ass off and people noticed. Now, he is one of the top plumbers in our area simply due to hard work and mindset.

Anyone of us can achieve whatever status we want in life. Most people are completely satisfied to live an average, "normal" life and complain about how rough they have it. Just as the obese person will not change their diet and exercise or the alcoholic will not put the bottle down, the working poor will not change anything in their lives. They will do the same thing they have always done and get the same results that they always have and look in disbelief like something should have changed by now.

Well, guess what? The only one who can change you, your attitude and your mindset is you; no one else can do it. Only you have the control and power to make that change and unfortunately, most of you never will.

We are also taught in our lives that borrowing is the only way to get anything we really need or want. We are taught to borrow for vehicles, homes, appliances, furniture, and education. We are told if we want to have nice "stuff" or get ahead, this is how we do it. I just wish there was a class that told what a load of bullshit this really is.

The bad thing is most of the people teaching the mindset of borrowing to buy this or buy that have no idea how stupid it really is. They have all fallen under the same spell and illusion of "stuff." The only way we are going to ever fix this is to change our mindset.

We have got to start with our kids in our homes and in our schools to let them know they don't need all this "stuff" that the world says they should have. But the problem is we have to start by example. That means we have to be willing to give up the things we can't afford.

Quit buying cars we can't afford every couple of years or quit financing furniture, appliances, TVs and all the other things we do. We say we want our kids to have a life better than we did, but we are teaching them to have it worse. We are teaching them to value "stuff" and expect debt as a normal. It makes my head hurt just to think about it.

Hard work most definitely pays off! Just as the example I gave with my brother a little bit ago and his plumbing business. And almost every successful person out there has their own story. We have to work hard and be dedicated. We have to find out what we do best and then go out and do it better than anyone else. We have to get noticed for what we can do and set ourselves apart from the crowd.

That's what successful people do. They don't care about what everyone else has or what everyone else is doing.

Did you know Warren Buffett lives in the same house he originally bought in 1958 for $31,500? Yes, he's most definitely done some renovations and updates I'm sure, but my point is he is not worried about "stuff." This is a man who could literally buy or build any house, any size and anywhere in the entire world and he is happy as a lark living in his original home bought in 1958 in Oklahoma. Omaha, NE

I bet that just made at least of few of your stomach's turn. Here we are wanting a new house every few years, wanting new cars every few years and never satisfied and one of the wealthiest men in the world lives in a home he gave $31,500 for. That is the true definition of being content.

But this is the stuff they don't teach in our school systems. Just as the older friend of mine told me years ago, "Until you can find contentment and be happy with what you have today you will never be able to be successful in life." These words need to echo in our ears every time we decide to do something dumb and buy something we don't need.

Starting Young

I know I said it before, but I want to beat this into your minds. We have got to start our kids young at changing their mindset. We need to let them know it's okay to fail, actually it's part of life, but to get back up, dust themselves off and learn from that failure. We need to let them know that not everyone is a winner in this life. There are losers and there are winners and most of the time we get to choose which one we will be.

We need to teach our kids about investing. We need them to understand that time is of the essence and that the sooner they begin investing, the wealthier they will be at a younger age. We need to teach them that giving is a key element in being financially successful and saving, "not spending" is the glue that holds it all together. We have got to get our kids fired up about not being okay with being "normal." To help them understand that being different is actually a better way of life.

When people tell me they can't be rich or they will never have a chance at being a millionaire, I typically just laugh. You want to get someone fired up just give a little chuckle when they make a stupid statement like that. It fires them up because they want me to agree with them like somehow, they are the one that broke the mold. Like they are somehow the one person that saving, investing, patience and time won't work for.

What a load of crap! Of course, it will work for them. What they are really saying when they make statements like that is, "Well, I am not willing to put any effort in at all into being a millionaire. I like having nice stuff, driving fancy cars and a big house. I like people seeing everything I've got and them being jealous of it. I like people thinking I've made it even though I am in debt up to my eyeballs."

That is what they are really saying when they say they have no chance of being a millionaire. It's not that they don't have the chance; it's that they choose not to be a millionaire. They choose to live just like they are and not change. You know quite honestly, I would much rather them just come out and tell me that they just aren't willing to change. At least then I would respect them more for their honesty. But we live in a society where we don't take personal responsibility, I almost forgot!

If you want to win, win. If you don't, then continue on the path of spending, instant gratification and "stuff" while blaming everyone else for your financial problems. Whether you believe it or not the choice is yours!

So I ask you; which choice will you make today? Will you go on through life blaming others for your misfortunes? Will you continue to want "stuff" so badly that you will get it at any costs? Will you sacrifice you and your family's well-being for the next newest widget? Or, will you take a stand today; learn from my experiences and my mistakes and *CHOOSE TO WIN!*

CONCLUSION

Well, if you made it to the end of this book, good for you! And I truly mean that. But reading a book is only the start. I remember the first financial book I ever read. It was called *Rich Dad Poor Dad* by Robert Kiyosaki and Sharon Lechter. (I recommend reading it.)

But one of the things it said in the book was, if you didn't believe you could do this at this point in your life, (it was talking about investing,) that it was only a pipe dream and to just put the book down and move on.

I am using a paraphrase, of course, but I would say basically the same here. If you read this book and you are still saying I can't do this, then you basically wasted a few hours of your life that you could have used to watch TV. Sucks for you!

On the other hand, if you read this book and are thinking, "If this guy can do it, so can I," then good for you. I couldn't agree with you more and I would love to hear your story once you do it.

I don't believe I am a genius by any means, but I have had enough experiences to know things that work and things that do not. As I have stated in this book many times, being financially free is a mindset and a choice.

If your head is not right, you will not succeed. You cannot blame others and others cannot be held responsible for your stupid decisions. Get off the couch, quit watching TV and do something with your life. Make a change! No one on this earth is going to make it for you.

If you have friends that are holding you back, get rid of them. If they think this kind of thing is stupid, then it's time to make new friends. You become the people you hang around with.

Find friends with the same interest. Find people who are financially successful and pick their brains. Buy them lunch or a cup of coffee and ask them how they did it. You will find most of them will love to share their story.

Get rid of the bad habits you have. Be content! Quit wanting every new widget or car that comes on the market and be satisfied. Decide today that tomorrow is going to be different. Believe in yourself and your abilities.

Don't let anyone else control who you become just because they choose not to WIN.

Value your time and not "stuff." Understand that time is the most important asset you have and be wise who you donate it too. Only volunteer your time to people who value it, not people who use it. Make time for your family and don't worry about what other people say or think.

Most people will think you are weird. They will not understand the change in your life and even when you try to explain it, they still will not get it.

If you haven't started investing, then figure out what you need to do in order to begin. Pay off your debts first, get an emergency fund and then begin investing. It is key to being financially successful. Until your money works for you, you will never really be financially free.

Help your kids be different than the other kids. Begin talking about this stuff young so they can grow up with a different mindset than you did. Help change their thought process and show them that being different with money is a good thing. Help them to understand that buying into the world's view of "normal" and "stuff" is simply financial self-destruction.

Get to a place in life where you can give back to people. Get to a place where you desire to help people and give to charities. It is such a satisfying place and it will help you realize and be grateful for what you have.

Again, I really appreciate you reading this book and I hope in some way this helps you begin your journey to Financial Freedom!

ACKNOWLEDGMENTS

One of the greatest men I ever knew was a man by the name of Bill Horne. He was my college professor and a writer for our local paper. A few days before he passed away in 2010, he wrote an article titled "Be Grateful for Our Greatest Gift."

His entire article can be summed up in a few words: Value your time, don't put so much emphasis on "stuff" and shiny things, be kind to people and give back, dream big and start young, and always cherish time spent with family. These are all things I wish I would have put more emphasis on earlier in my life.

I have had many experiences in my life that have allowed me to succeed and fail. But I finally realized that failing was just a stepping stone to success.

Choosing to WIN with Financial Freedom has many stories of my personal failures and successes. I have shared personal stories that I hope can, in some way, help contribute to someone else's success and help them avoid some of their own failures.

This book would not have even been possible without the many people that have inspired me along the way; from my previous business partners, professors, close friends, and even a few competitors.

I would like to give special acknowledgment to a few individuals.

First and foremost, I would like to thank my wife, Felicity Patton. Without her standing beside me through most of these failures, there would have never been the successes to tell about. Her dedication and love are second to none.

I would like to thank my brother, Bret, who has always been someone that is willing to give me honest and constructive criticism. Bret also helped me with different ideas and gave me a lot of input and feedback in the writing process.

I would like to also thank my aunt Donna, who is also an author, and was willing to help me through the editing process of this book as well as helping me get this book to market.

And lastly, I would like to thank my parents, Bud and Karen, for always being there for me no matter what. Even though we didn't have a lot of money growing up, we always had what we needed and most importantly, we always had love.

ABOUT THE AUTHOR

Josh Patton is an entrepreneur and investor who continues to focus on his real estate brokerage as well as his real estate investing and development company.

Josh and his wife, Felicity, have been married since 2001 and have three daughters.

Josh began his real estate career in 2006 and opened his own real estate brokerage in February of 2011.

Josh has owned a diversity of investments that include: stocks, bonds, mutual funds, residential and commercial real estate, and more.

Josh grew up in a poor, but loving family, and credits that to why he was able to be successful in his life.

"Hard work and perseverance has made me the man I am today."

"I simply try to live my life and teach our children to live their lives without putting so much emphasis on stuff."

"I have learned over the years to value time as much as you can because it is a limited resource and your most precious asset."

"I hope this book not only inspires you but motivates you to quit living a life that is a slave to 'stuff.'

I would like for everyone who has read *Choosing to Win with Financial Freedom*, to begin taking control of their own finances. I hope that after you have read this book, you get up, get motivated, and CHOOSE to WIN!"

CPSIA information can be obtained
at www.ICGtesting.com
Printed in the USA
FFHW022145100219
50509994-55764FF

9 780692 122167